Modes of Writing
NARRATIVES

Richard Andrews and Angela Fisher

Series editor: Richard Andrews

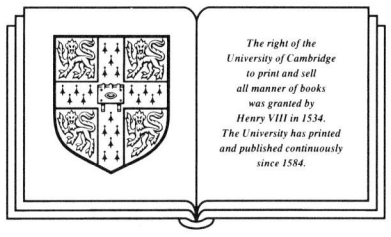

Cambridge University Press

Cambridge
New York   Port Chester
Melbourne   Sydney

Published by the Press Syndicate of the University of Cambridge
The Pitt Building, Trumpington Street, Cambridge CB2 IRP
40 West 20th Street, New York, NY 10011-4211, USA
10 Stamford Road, Oakleigh, Victoria 3166, Australia

© Cambridge University Press 1991

First published 1991

Printed in Great Britain by Scotprint Ltd, Musselburgh

A catalogue record for this book is available from the British Library

ISBN 0 521 39968 8 paperback

Produced by Zoë Books Limited
15, Worthy Lane, Winchester,
Hampshire SO23 7AB

Designed by Sterling Associates
Artwork by Linda Combi
Picture Research by Valerie Randall

Cover design by Linda Combi

NOTICE TO TEACHERS

The contents of this book are in the copyright of Cambridge University Press or the named authors. Unauthorised copying of any of the pages is not only illegal but also goes against the interests of the authors. For authorised copying please check that your school has a licence (through the local education authority) from the Copyright Licensing Agency which enables you to copy small parts of the text in limited numbers.

MODES OF WRITING

Modes of Writing is a series which aims to bring a wide range of writing to the attention of students aged fourteen and upwards. It consists of three anthologies: *Narratives*, *Arguments* and *Descriptions*.

Narratives is a collection of stories, anecdotes, tales, comic strips, myths, fables and letters, all of which depend on the linking of events and states of mind in a sequence. The sequence takes place in time, though the 'events' may not necessarily be told in chronological order. Indeed, one of the points of this collection is to show that playing with time rather than simply representing time in writing is what narrative enables us to do. Another of the intentions here is to make it clear that narrative can be used not only to tell one's own story (as in autobiography), or in fiction, but also to record scientific observations, to argue a case (as in fables) and as a way of thinking.

Arguments includes everything from letters by Groucho Marx to a letter from a parent to a headteacher about school uniform; from cartoons to travel writing; from poems to a Monty Python script. Here it is the putting over of a point of view that is the focus rather than the telling of a sequence of events. The interrelationship of ideas is of more interest than the relationship with time. People are using language to persuade others to adopt their point of view, and they are using language in a much more varied way than the conventional 'essay' suggests (or allows).

The third book in the series, **Descriptions**, covers the range of writing which attempts to stay close to things in the world. Sometimes it uses narrative (as in reports), and at other times it argues a point simply through describing what it sees. On further occasions - in commentary, in conveying its subject matter in the present tense - it depends on neither of these methods, but appears to have a life of its own. It moves easily backwards and forwards between the 'real world' and the worlds of fiction (though it also sees the real world as one of a number of possible worlds).

If there appears to be a degree of overlap between these three books, that is part of the plan. These are not watertight categories with their own rules, but ways of organising writing which are flexible and which can be combined. Part of the aim of the series is to encourage invention, risk-taking and cross-over between these modes of composition, in 'English' and in other subjects.

By building the series on the principle of broad modes of writing rather than by themes or authors, we also draw attention to the different types of language that are available to writers as they compose. This is a series *about* language as well as one which is promoting the use of language in lively, productive and entertaining ways.

Lastly, we have wanted to produce books that are arguments in themselves: books which present a certain vision of the possibilities in language, but which are also there to argue with. To this end, we have tried to demystify the process of compiling the anthologies. We have demonstrated the thinking that has led to a particular choice of text or to a particular sequencing of texts. We hope that you will use these books critically: enter into a dialogue with the texts and go beyond the suggestions we have made in the activities.

Richard Andrews

CONTENTS

Introduction	6
Mini- and Micro-stories	7
A Better Place *Brett Lovell*	8
Saturday Shopping *Diana Rigg*	8
A Cautionary Tale of the Calorific Pitfalls on the Road to True Love *Penny Maplestone*	8
Winnie and Walter *Anonymous*	9
Freedom to Breathe *Alexander Solzhenitsyn*	10
Which of these are stories? *Various*	10
'Notation' *Raymond Queneau*	13
'Litotes' *Raymond Queneau*	13
'Interjections' *Raymond Queneau*	13
'Official Letter' *Raymond Queneau*	14
The Full Bus *John Cage*	15
On Discovery *Maxine Hong Kingston*	15
On Fathers *Maxine Hong Kingston*	16
The Captive *Jorge Luis Borges*	17
Cat in the Rain *Ernest Hemingway*	18
Tales which Teach	21
The Great Manito *Delaware Indians*	22
Why the Sky is Far Away *Bini people*	24
from the Popul Vuh *Mayan people*	24
A Story of Our Times *Pitika Ntuli*	25
Dog Digs to China *Linda Combi*	26
The North Wind and the Sun *La Fontaine*	27
The Chicks' Nest *Wu Guangxiao*	27
The Two Clay Men *Du Li*	27
Two Feminist Fables *Suniti Namjoshi*	28
Anecdotes of Mr Keuner: Good Turns *Bertolt Brecht*	29
The Woodcutter's Son *Fred Manley*	30
Images towards Story-Writing *Linda Combi*	36
The Voice on the Page	37
Timelines *Gabriel Swartland and Amy Strickland*	38
'Everyone thought he was cool and tough ...' *Linda Haas*	40
The Projectile *Raymond Carver*	41
Testament of a Little Doffer *Elizabeth Bentley*	42
'I have to be a waitress ...' *Dolores Dante*	44
Family Snaps	46
John *John Best*	47
'I used to think babies ...' *Iris Bradford*	48
The Toilet *Gcina Mhlope*	49

A Recollection *Frances Cornford*	55
Blind Date *Bob Clarke*	56
Learning to Stalk Muskrats *Annie Dillard*	58
Service Wash *Victoria Wood*	59

This is How it Was — 61

True Stories *Christopher Logue*	62
'I was on a bus to Washington, D.C. ...' *Tobias Wolff*	63
Solo Tackle *Ramon Figueroa*	63
Travelling in a Comfortable Car *Bertolt Brecht*	64
The Fire of London *Samuel Pepys*	65
A Prize-Fight *Samuel Pepys*	65
Working from a Photograph *Pete Skingley*	66
Comparative Methods of Medicine *Ousama*	67
Ingrafting the Small-pox *Lady Mary Wortley Montagu*	67
Description of Cells *Robert Hooke*	68
Photojournalism	70
Letter from a Diplomat to his Wife *Harold Nicolson*	71
Extract from a Journal Kept Whilst in Hospital *Angela Fisher*	71
The Indian Rebellion *Adelaide Case*	72
One Less Octopus at Paxos *Russell Hoban*	73
South African Journal *Barbara Webb*	74

Short Stories — 77

1997: The Illegal Immigrant *Isobel Jacobs*	78
Nicole and the Giant Cake *Celia Milford*	79
The Follower *Cynthia Asquith*	84
Thank You, M'am *Langston Hughes*	87
The Story of an Hour *Kate Chopin*	90
The Blue Bouquet *Octavio Paz*	92
An Unpleasant Reminder *Anna Kavan*	94
A Story to Finish *George Orwell*	96
What a Beauty! *Theo van den Boogaard*	100

Activities — 101

List of Texts by Theme — 125

Index of Authors and Illustrators — 127

INTRODUCTION

Stories are compelling: if someone starts one in a far corner of the room, we find ourselves being drawn towards it. We might even break off our conversation with someone else and actually move towards it. And until the story is finished, we cannot get away. It would be almost impossible to leave in the middle.

We are moved by stories. We love listening to them. Why is this?

One of the reasons is that stories take us on a journey. They give us all the pleasures of travel without our having to go anywhere. Sometimes we do not know where the journey is going to end, though we have a rough idea of how long it will take. Every step on the way is new and although we can look back over our shoulder to see where we have come from, we enjoy the suspense of not knowing exactly where we are going. But when we get to the end of the journey - if the story has been a good one - we arrive with a satisfied feeling. At other times, we know where the story is going to end, because we have heard it before. The pleasures are different this time: we know where the journey will end, so we can enjoy the sights on the way and the pleasures of the landmarks.

Stories are one form of narrative - the umbrella term that covers told stories, novels, anecdotes, scientific accounts, autobiographies and biographies, comic strips, some jokes and some films. Any form that consists of a sequence of events or thoughts or feelings in time can be called a narrative. The sequence need not be strictly chronological (for example, films and stories that have flashbacks) but it is usually set in time. Narrative (from the Latin *narrare*, meaning to tell or to relate) almost always involves a teller with a point of view. Sometimes the teller introduces himself or herself; at other times he or she is distant from us.

Why do we need to tell stories? Why do we need narrative?

Often, things do not make sense to us unless we can think of them in story form. Stories and other narratives are one of the ways we can remember and share common experience, and in this respect they can act as a bond in our society - whether it be amongst the family, a group of friends or in the society as a whole. History is a set of such stories.

Stories can also have personal significance. We see our lives in terms of a story with a beginning and an end. We run narratives in our heads in order to explain things to ourselves; and we make up stories of how things might turn out.

One of the marvellous things about stories is that they can be either real or fictional. Sometimes it is very hard to tell the difference, and sometimes it does not matter. Whether they are real or fictional, stories always chart possible worlds, and enable us to work out what we would do if we found ourselves in those worlds.

Stories and other narratives can be spoken or written, listened to and read. They can be as short as a few words or stretch to millions. Most of those we have collected in this book are relatively short, and we have tried to cover as wide a range as possible. We hope you enjoy them!

Angela Fisher and Richard Andrews

MINI- AND MICRO-STORIES

A Better Place

We're going to a better place, me, Abraham and our children. I crowded in this train but that doesn't matter, we're going to a better place but first we have to shower. Only once they were in the showers did they realise they really were going to a better place.

Brett Lovell

Saturday Shopping

Home at last, light the gas fire, fill the kettle. All that planning has paid off. Silly women acting on impulse always got caught. Not her. Life would be different now, have some meaning. The bundle in the holdall stirred. Rock it gently. "Sssh little love, you are mine now..."

Diana Rigg

A Cautionary Tale of the Calorific Pitfalls on the Road to True Love

Hasn't phoned yet. Peanut butter sandwich. Don't see why I should. Jam doughnut. Doesn't love me anymore. Half *baguette*, brie and pickled onion. Probably out with someone thinner. Is there cheesecake in the freezer? I will not phone. Just one square of chocolate. Ring ring. Hiya, meet me for dinner?

Penny Maplestone

Winnie and Walter

"Warm weather Walter! Welcome warm weather! We were wishing winter would wane, weren't we?"

"We were well wearied of waiting," whispered Walter wearily. Wan, white, woe-begone was Walter, wayward, wilful, worn with weakness, wasted, waxing weaker whenever winter's wild, withering winds were wailing. Wholly without waywardness was Winifred, Walter's wise, womanly watcher, who, with winsome, wooing way, was well-beloved.

"We won't wait, Walter; while the weather's warm we'll wander where woodlands wave, won't we?"

Walter's wanton wretchedness wholly waned. "Why, Winnie, we'll walk where we went when we were with Willie; we'll weave wildflower wreaths, watch woodmen working, woodlice, worms wriggling, windmills whirling, watermills wheeling; we will win wild whortleberries, witness wheat winnowed."

Wisbeach woods were wild with wildflowers; warm, westerly winds whispered where willows were waving; wood-pigeons, wrens, woodpeckers were warbling wild woodnotes. Where Wisbeach watermill's waters, which were wholly waveless, widened, were water-lilies, waxen white. Winifred wove wreaths with woodbine, whitehorn, wallflowers, whilst Walter whittled wooden wedges with willow wands.

Wholly without warning, wild wet winds woke within Wisbeach woods, whistling where Winifred wandered with Walter; weeping willows were wailing weirdly; waging war with wind-tossed waters. Winifred's wary watchfulness waked.

"Walter we won't wait."

"Which way, Winnie?"

Winifred wavered. "Why, where were we wandering? Wisbeach woods widen whichever way we walk; where's Wisbeach white wicket; where's Winston's water-mill?"

Wistfully, Walter witnessed Winifred's wonder. "Winnie, Winnie, we were wrong, wholly wrong, wandering within wild ways. Wayfaring weather-beaten waifs, well-nigh worn out."

Winifred waited where, within wattled woodwork walls, wagons, wheelbarrows, wains were waiting, weighty with withered wood. Walter, warmly wrapped with Winifred's well-worn wadded waterproof, was wailing woefully, wholly wearied. Winnie, who, worn with watching, well-nigh weeping, was wistfully, wakefully waiting Willie's well-known whistle, wholly wished Walter's well-being warranted.

With well-timed wisdom, Walter was wound with wide worsted wrappers, which wonderfully well withstood winter's withering whistling winds. Wholly without warm wrappers was Winifred, who, with womanly wisdom, was watching Walter's welfare, warding Walter's weakness.

"When will Willie wend where we wait?" wearily wondered Walter.

"Whist, Walter," whispered Winnie, "who was whooping?"
"Whereabouts?"

Welcome whistling was waking Wisbeach woods when winter's windy warfare waxed weaker.

"Winnie! Walter!"

Winifred's wakefulness was well-grounded. "We're well Willie; we're where Winston's wagons wait."

Without waiting, Willie was within Winston's woodwork walls.

"Welcome, welcome Willie." Winnie was weeping with weariness with watching Walter, weak with wayfaring.

"Why, Winnie! Wise, watchful, warm-hearted Winnie," Willie whispered wheedlingly. "We won't weep, Walter's well. What were Walter without Winnie?

Wholly wonderful was Winifred's well-timed womanly wisdom, which well warranted weakly Walter's welfare. Whenever wandering within Wisbeach woods with Winnie, Walter would whisper, "What were Walter without Winnie? Wise, watchful, warmhearted Winnie!"

Anonymous

Freedom to Breathe

A shower fell in the night and now dark clouds drift across the sky, occasionally sprinkling a fine film of rain.

I stand under an apple-tree in blossom and I breathe. Not only the apple-tree but the grass round it glistens with moisture; words cannot describe the sweet fragrance that pervades the air. Inhaling as deeply as I can, the aroma invades my whole being; I breathe with my eyes open, I breathe with my eyes closed - I cannot say which gives me the greater pleasure.

This, I believe, is the single most precious freedom that prison takes away from us: the freedom to breathe freely, as I now can. No food on earth, no wine, not even a woman's kiss is sweeter to me than this air steeped in the fragrance of flowers, of moisture and freshness.

No matter that this is only a tiny garden, hemmed in by five-storey houses like cages in a zoo. I cease to hear the motorcycles backfiring, the radios whining, the burble of loudspeakers. As long as there is fresh air to breathe under an apple-tree after a shower, we may survive a little longer.

Alexander Solzhenitsyn

Which of these are stories?

I   I have been sent on errands to our Colonies on many planets. Crises of all kinds are familiar to me. I have been involved in emergencies that threaten species, or carefully planned local programmes. I have known more than once, what it is to accept failure, final and irreversible of an effort or experiment to do with creatures who have within themselves the potential of development dreamed of, planned for ... and then - Finis! The end! The drum pattering out into silence ...

II Ken Jones was a shop steward
in a warehouse in Liverpool.
He had a parrot at work.
He was working with a checker.
The parrot told the checker to stuff it.
The checker had the parrot for tea.
He told Ken it was not too bad.

III Sunday - wash car, garage and roof of garage
Monday - read the complete works of Shakespeare
Tuesday - go for a hospital check-up
Wednesday - supermarket: remember butter, cakes, cream, cheeses
Thursday - read the Bible
Friday - sleep
Saturday - wash underside of car, polish garage

IV Vibrant with music, with magic, with the knowledge of age-old mysteries as well as fresh injustice, here is the saga of two Native American families, told with authenticity unmatched in contemporary fiction. As the destinies of the Kashpaws and the Lamartines touch, ignite and explode on a North Dakota reservation, the death of one extraordinary Chippewa woman becomes the flash point for old memories, new truths, and secrets whose time has come. In lives crowded with tragedy and comedy, strong-willed men and women find themselves bound by all the forms of love: the endlessly true snag of the flesh, the bind of blood, the union that begins in white-heat and ends in betrayal ...

V American planes, full of holes and wounded men and corpses took off backwards from an airfield in England. Over France, a few German fighter planes flew at them backwards, sucked bullets and shell fragments from some of the planes and crewmen. They did the same for the wrecked American bombers on the ground, and those planes flew up backwards to join the formation.
   The formation flew backwards over a German city that was in flames. The bombers opened up their bomb bay doors, exerted a miraculous magnetism which shrunk the fires, gathered them into cylindrical steel containers and lifted the containers into the bellies of the planes. The containers were stored neatly in racks.The Germans below had miraculous devices of their own, which were long steel tubes. They used them to suck more fragments from the crewmen and planes. But there were still a few wounded Americans, though, and some of the bombers were in bad repair. Over France, though,

German fighters came up again, made everything and everybody as good as new.

VI   The country described. A proposal for correcting modern maps. The King's Palace, and some account of the metropolis. The author's way of travelling. The chief temple described.

VII   A slumber did my spirit seal
      I had no human fears:
She seem'd a thing that could not feel
      The touch of earthly years.

No motion has she now, no force;
      She neither hears nor sees,
Roll'd round in earth's diurnal course
      With rocks and stones and trees!

VIII   I spent most of the morning trying to find the house that the estate agent had directed me to. When I got there a woman opened the door and immediately began complaining to me about the state of the street. I took a quick look round the house, then she let us into the backyard. We got locked out of the house by the wind which blew the door to. There was no way out into the back lane, as that door was locked too. I found a step-ladder and tried to climb back in through the little window. I got half way in, then found that the crotch of my trousers had got caught on the little thing that sticks up to secure the window catch. I couldn't move, and was afraid I was doing myself an injury. She shouted for help from a neighbour, but no one could get into the yard. I tried to fall into the room, but only got myself more impaled on the little spike. Then I heard the front door open. It was her husband

IX   The hunter is chasing the tiger through the mountains. The tiger reaches a river and begs a tortoise to carry him across the river on his back. The tortoise, being kindhearted, carries the tiger across the stream. Arriving at the other bank, the tiger says, "Friend, since there is no food here and I am hungry, let me eat you." The tortoise withdraws into his shell and no matter how hard the tiger tries he can't crack it open.

    As each day passes, the tiger becomes hungrier. Finally he pleads with the tortoise, "Please carry me back across the river."

X   There was a man walking down the street with a cabbage on a lead. Another man came along and said, "Why have you got that cabbage on a lead?".

    "Cabbage?" said the first man, " The man in the pet shop told me it was a collie."

XI Thorfast would probably have made combs. Once he had cut out the pieces of antler for making the comb he would then smooth them down and fix all the individual parts together by using small metal nails. The comb-maker would then decorate the comb's plates with various geometric patterns, after which he cut out the comb's teeth using a fine saw.

otation

In the S bus, in the rush hour. A chap of about 26, felt hat with a cord instead of a ribbon, neck too long, as if someone's been having a tug-of-war with it. People getting off. The chap in question gets annoyed with one of the men standing next to him. He accuses him of jostling him every time anyone goes past. A snivelling tone which is meant to be aggressive. When he sees a vacant seat he throws himself on to it.

Two hours later, I meet him in the Cour de Rome, in front of the gare Saint-Lazare. He's with a friend who's saying: "You ought to get an extra button put on your overcoat." He shows him where (at the lapels) and why.

itotes

Some of us were travelling together. A young man, who didn't look very intelligent, spoke to the man next to him for a few moments then he went and sat down. Two hours later I met him again; he was with a friend and was talking about clothes.

nterjections

Psst! h'm! ah! oh! hem! ah! ha! hey! well!
oh! pooh! poof! ow! oo! ouch! hey! eh!
h'm! pffft!
Well! hey! pooh! oh! h'm! right!

fficial Letter

I beg to advise you of the following facts of which I happened to be the equally impartial and horrified witness.

Today, at roughly twelve noon, I was present on the platform of a bus which was proceeding up the rue de Courcelles in the direction of the Place Champerret. The aforementioned bus was fully laden - more than fully laden, I might even venture to say, since the conductor had accepted an overload of several candidates, without valid reason and actuated by an exaggerated kindness of heart which caused him to exceed the regulations and which, consequently, bordered on indulgence. At each stopping place the perambulations of the outgoing and incoming passengers did not fail to provoke a certain disturbance which incited one of these passengers to protest, though not without timidity. I should mention that he went and sat down as and when this eventually became possible.

I will append to this short account this addendum: I had occasion to observe this passenger some time subsequently in the company of an individual whom I was unable to identify. The conversation which they were exchanging with some animation seemed to have a bearing on questions of an aesthetic nature.

In view of these circumstances, I would request you to be so kind, Sir, as to intimate to me the inference which I should draw from these facts and the attitude which you would then deem appropriate that I adopt in re the conduct of my subsequent mode of life.

Anticipating the favour of your reply, believe me to be, Sir, your very obedient servant at least.

Raymond Queneau

The Full Bus

A crowded bus on the point of leaving Manchester for Stockport was found by its conductress to have one too many standees. She therefore asked, "Who was the last person to get on the bus?" No one said a word. Declaring that the bus would not leave until the extra passenger was put off, she went and fetched the driver, who also asked, "All right, who was the last person to get on the bus?" Again there was a public silence. So the two went to find an inspector. He asked, "Who was the last person to get on the bus?" No one spoke. He then announced that he would fetch a policeman. While the conductress, driver and inspector were away looking for a policeman, a little man came up to the bus stop and asked, "Is this the bus to Stockport?" Hearing that it was, he got on. A few minutes later the three returned accompanied by a policeman. He asked, "What seems to be the trouble? Who was the last person to get on the bus?" The little man said, "I was." The policeman said, "All right, get off." All the people on the bus burst into laughter. The conductress, thinking they were laughing at her, burst into tears and said she refused to make the trip to Stockport. The inspector then arranged for another conductress to take over. She, seeing the little man standing at the bus stop, said, "What are you doing there?" He said, "I'm waiting to go to Stockport." She said, "Well, this is the bus to Stockport. Are you getting on or not?"

John Cage

On Discovery

Once upon a time, a man, named Tang Ao, looking for the Gold Mountain, crossed an ocean, and came upon the Land of Women. The women immediately captured him, not on guard against ladies. When they asked Tang Ao to come along, he followed; if he had had male companions, he would've winked over his shoulder.

"We have to prepare you to meet the queen," the women said. They locked him in a canopied apartment equipped with pots of makeup, mirrors, and a woman's clothes. "Let us help you off with your armour and boots," said the women. They slipped his coat off his shoulders, pulled it down his arms, and shackled his wrists behind him. The women who kneeled to take off his shoes chained his ankles together.

A door opened, and he expected to meet his match, but it was only two old women with sewing boxes in their hands. "The less you struggle, the less it'll hurt," one said, squinting a bright eye as she threaded her needle. Two captors sat on him while another held his head. He felt an old woman's dry fingers trace his ear; the long nail on her little finger scraped his neck. "What are you doing?" he asked. "Sewing your lips together," she joked, blackening needles in a candle flame. The ones who sat on him bounced with laughter. But the old women did not sew his lips together. They pulled his earlobes taut and jabbed a needle through each of them. They had to poke and probe before puncturing the layers of skin correctly, the hole in the front of the lobe in line with the one in back, the layers of skin sliding about so. They worked the needle through - a last jerk for the needle's wide eye ('needle's nose' in Chinese). They strung his raw flesh with silk threads; he could feel the fibres.

The women who sat on him turned to direct their attention to his feet. They bent his toes so far backwards that his arched foot cracked. The old ladies squeezed each foot and broke many tiny bones along the sides. They gathered his toes over and under one another like a knot of ginger root. Tang Ao wept with pain. As they wound the bandages tight and tighter around his feet, the women sang footbinding songs to distract him: "Use aloe for binding feet and not for scholars."

During the months of a season, they fed him on women's food: the tea was thick with white chrysanthemums and stirred the cool female winds inside his body; chicken wings made his hair shine; vinegar soup improved his womb. They drew the loops of thread through the scabs that grew daily over the holes in his earlobes. One day they inserted gold hoops. Every night they unbound his feet, but his veins had shrunk, and the blood pumping through them hurt so much, he begged to have his feet re-wrapped tight. They forced him to wash his used bandages, which were embroidered with flowers and smelled of rot and cheese. He hung the bandages up to dry, streamers that drooped and draped wall to wall. He felt embarrassed; the wrappings were like underwear, and they were his.

One day his attendants changed his gold hoops to jade studs and strapped his feet to shoes that curved like bridges. They plucked out each hair on his face, powdered him white, painted his eyebrows like a moth's wings, painted his cheeks and lips red. He served a meal at the queen's court. His hips swayed and his shoulders swivelled because of his shaped feet. "She's pretty, don't you agree?" the diners said, smacking their lips at his dainty feet as he bent to put dishes before them.

On Fathers

Waiting at the gate for our father to come home from work, my brothers and sisters and I saw a man come hastening around the corner. Father! "BaBa!" "BaBa!" We flew off the gate; we jumped off the fence. "Baba!" We surrounded him, took his hands, pressed our noses against his coat to sniff his tobacco smell, reached into his pockets for the Rainbo notepads and the gold coins that were really chocolates. The littlest ones hugged his legs for a ride on his shoes.

And he laughed a startled laugh. "But I'm not your father. You've made a mistake." He took our hands out of his pockets. "But I'm not your father." Looking closely, we saw that he probably was not. We went back inside the yard, and this man continued his walk down our street, from the back certainly looking like our father, one hand in his pocket. Tall and thin, he was wearing our father's two-hundred-dollar suit that fit him just right. He was walking fast in his good leather shoes with the wingtips.

Our mother came out of the house, and we hung on to her while she explained, "No, that wasn't your father. He did look like BaBa, though, didn't he? From the back, almost exactly." We stood on the sidewalk together and watched the man walk away. A moment later, from the other direction, our own father came striding towards us, the one finger touching his hat to salute us. We ran again to meet him.

Maxine Hong Kingston

The Captive

This story is told out in one of the old frontier towns - either Junín or Tapalquén. A boy was missing after an Indian raid; it was said that the marauders had carried him away. The boy's parents searched for him without any luck; years later, a soldier just back from Indian territory told them about a blue-eyed savage who may have been their son. At long last they traced him (the circumstances of the search have not come down to us and I dare not invent what I don't know) and they thought they recognized him. The man, marked by the wilderness and by primitive life, no longer understood the words of the language he spoke in childhood, but he let himself be led, uncurious and willing, to his old house. There he stopped - maybe because the others stopped. He stared at the door as though not understanding what it was. All of a sudden, ducking his head, he let out a cry, cut through the entranceway and the two long patios on the run, and burst into the kitchen. Without a second's pause, he buried his arm in the soot-blackened oven chimney and drew out the small knife with the horn handle that he had hidden there as a boy. His eyes lit up with joy and his parents wept because they had found their lost child.

Maybe other memories followed upon this one, but the Indian could not live indoors and one day he left to go back to his open spaces. I would like to know what he felt in that first bewildering moment in which past and present merged; I would like to know whether in that dizzying instant the lost son was born again and died, or whether he managed to recognize, as child or a dog might, his people and his home.

Jorge Luis Borges

Cat in the Rain

There were only two Americans stopping at the hotel. They did not know any of the people they passed on the stairs on their way to and from their room. Their room was on the second floor facing the sea. It also had the public garden and the war monument. There were big palms and green benches in the public garden. In the good weather there was always an artist with his easel. Artists liked the way the palms grew and the bright colors of the hotels facing the gardens and the sea. Italians came from a long way off to look up at the war monument. It was made of bronze and glistened in the rain. It was raining. The rain dripped from the palm trees. Water stood in pools on the gravel paths. The sea broke in a long line in the rain and slipped back down the beach to come up and break again in a long line in the rain. The motor cars were gone from the square by the war monument. Across the square in the doorway of the cafe a waiter stood looking out at the empty square.

The American wife stood at the window looking out. Outside right under their window a cat was crouched under one of the dripping green tables. The cat was trying to make herself so compact that she would not be dripped on.

"I'm going down and get that kitty," the American wife said.

"I'll do it," her husband offered from the bed.

"No, I'll get it. The poor kitty out trying to keep dry under a table."

The husband went on reading, lying propped up with the two pillows at the foot of the bed.

"Don't get wet," he said.

The wife went downstairs and the hotel owner stood up and bowed to her as she passed the office. His desk was at the far end of the office. He was an old man and very tall.

"Il piove," the wife said. She liked the hotel-keeper.

"Si, si, Signora, brutto tempo. It's very bad weather."

He stood behind his desk in the far end of the dim room. The wife liked him. She liked the deadly serious way he received any compliments. She liked his dignity. She liked the way he wanted to serve her. She liked the way he felt about being a hotel-keeper. She liked his old, heavy face and big hands.

Liking him she opened the door and looked out. It was raining harder. A man in a rubber cape was crossing the empty square to the café. The cat would be around to the right. Perhaps she could go along under the eaves. As she stood in the doorway an umbrella opened behind her. It was the maid who looked after their room.

"You must not get wet," she smiled, speaking Italian. Of course, the hotel-keeper had sent her.

With the maid holding the umbrella over her, she walked along the gravel path until she was under their window. The table was there, washed bright green in the rain, but the cat was gone. She was suddenly disappointed. The maid looked up at her.

"Ha perduto qualque cosa, Signora?"

"There was a cat," said the American girl.

"A cat?"

"Si, il gatto."

"A cat?" the maid laughed. "A cat in the rain?"

"Yes," she said, "under the table." Then, "Oh, I wanted it so much. I wanted a kitty."

When she talked English the maid's face tightened.

"Come, Signora," she said. "We must get back inside. You will be wet."

"I suppose so," said the American girl.

They went back along the gravel path and passed in the door. The maid stayed outside to close the umbrella. As the American girl passed the office, the padrone bowed from his desk. Something felt very small and tight inside the girl. The padrone made her feel very small and at the same time really important. She had a momentary feeling of being of supreme importance. She went on up the stairs. She opened the door of the room. George was on the bed, reading.

"Did you get the cat?" he asked, putting the book down.

"It was gone."

"Wonder where it went to," he said, resting his eyes from reading.

She sat down on the bed.

"I wanted it so much," she said. "I don't know why I wanted it so much. I wanted that poor kitty. It isn't any fun to be a poor kitty out in the rain."

George was reading again.

She went over and sat in front of the mirror of the dressing table looking at herself with the hand glass. She studied her profile, first one side and then the other. Then she studied the back of her head and her neck.

"Don't you think it would be a good idea if I let my hair grow out?" she asked, looking at her profile again.

George looked up and saw the back of her neck, clipped close like a boy's.

"I like it the way it is."

"I get so tired of it," she said. "I get so tired of looking like a boy."

George shifted his position in the bed. He hadn't looked away from her since she started to speak.

"You look pretty darn nice," he said.

She laid the mirror down on the dresser and went over to the window and looked out. It was getting dark.

"I want to pull my hair back tight and smooth and make a big knot at the back that I can feel," she said. "I want to have a kitty to sit on my lap and purr when I stroke her."

"Yeah," George said from the bed.

"And I want to eat at a table with my own silver and I want

candles. And I want it to be spring and I want to brush my hair out in front of the mirror and I want a kitty and I want some new clothes."

"Oh, shut up and get something to read," George said. He was reading again.

His wife was looking out of the window. It was quite dark now and still raining in the palm trees.

"Anyway, I want a cat," she said, "I want a cat. I want a cat now. If I can't have long hair or any fun, I can have a cat."

George was not listening. He was reading his book. His wife looked out of the window where the light had come on in the square.

Someone knocked at the door.

"Avanti," George said. He looked up from his book.

In the doorway stood the maid. She held a big tortoise-shell cat pressed tight against her and swung down against her body.

"Excuse me," she said, "the padrone asked me to bring this for the Signora."

Ernest Hemingway

TALES WHICH TEACH

The Great Manito: a jumbled text

 Upon the earth there was a huge mist and there was the Great Manito.

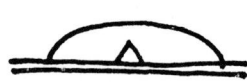 And groups of islands emerged and remained.

 Then the wind blew violently, it became lighter and water flowed strongly and from afar.

 But in great secrecy a spiteful creature, a power magician, appeared on earth.

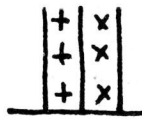 He made flies, he made mosquitoes.

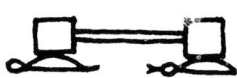 All this happened once upon a time on earth before the great flood, in the beginning.

 But a spiteful Manito made only spiteful creatures, monsters.

 In the beginning, at all times, above the earth, in this place.

 He made the huge earth and the sky.

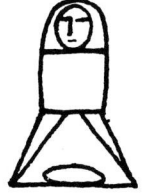 And thereafter he was the Manito of men and their grandfather.

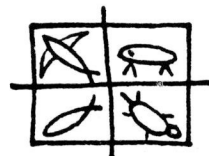 He sent fish, he sent turtles, he sent wild beasts, he sent birds.

 All creatures were friendly with one another at that time.

Tales which Teach 23

 Once again, the Great Manito spoke, one Manito to other Manitos.

 He made everything move in harmony.

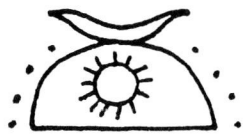 He made the sun, the moon and the stars.

 And they gave them to eat when they needed to.

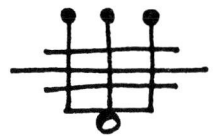 And with him brought unhappiness, quarrelling and misfortune.

 In the beginning, for ever, lost in space, was the Great Manito.

 Truly the Manitos were very active and considerate.

 Brought bad weather, brought sickness, brought death.

 To these first men of all and to these first mothers of all: they found them helpmeets.

 He sent the first mother, the mother of all creatures.

 All possessed joyful wisdom, all had time to spare and happiness.

 To mortal creatures, spirits and all.

Delaware Indians

Why the Sky is Far Away

In the beginning, the sky was very close to the earth. In those days men did not have to till the ground, because whenever they felt hungry they simply cut off a piece of the sky and ate it. But the sky grew angry, because often they cut off more than they could eat, and threw the left-overs on the rubbish heap. The sky did not want to be thrown on the rubbish heap, and so he warned men that if they were not more careful in future he would move far away.

For a while everyone paid attention to his warning. But one day a greedy woman cut off an enormous piece of the sky. She ate as much as she could, but was unable to finish it. Frightened, she called her husband, but he too could not finish it. They called the entire village to help, but they could not finish it. In the end they had to throw the remainder on the rubbish heap. Then the sky became very angry indeed, and rose up high above the earth, far beyond the reach of men. And from then on men have had to work for their living.

Bini people (Nigeria)

from the Popul Vuh

This is the account of how all was in suspense, all calm, in silence; all motionless, still, and the expanse of the sky was empty.

This is the first account, the first narrative. There was neither man, nor animal, birds, fishes, crabs, trees, stones, caves, ravines, grasses, nor forests; there was only the sky.

The surface of the earth had not appeared. There was only the calm sea and the great expanse of the sky.

There was nothing brought together, nothing which could make a noise, nor anything which might move, or tremble, or could make noise in the sky.

There was nothing standing; only the calm water, the placid sea, alone and tranquil. Nothing existed.

There was only immobility and silence in the darkness, in the night. Only the Creator, the Maker, Tepeu, Gucumatz, the Forefathers, were in the water surrounded with light. They were hidden under green and blue feathers, and were therefore called Gucumatz. By nature they were great sages and great thinkers. In this manner the sky existed and also the Heart of Heaven, which is the name of God and thus He is called.

Then came the word. Tepeu and Gucumatz came together in the darkness, in the night, and Tepeu and Gucumatz talked together. They talked then, discussing and deliberating; they agreed, they united their words and their thoughts.

Then while they meditated, it became clear to them that when dawn would break, man must appear. Then they planned the creation, and the growth of the trees and the thickets and the birth of life and the creation of man. Thus it was arranged in the darkness and in the night by the Heart of Heaven who is called Huracan.

The first is called Caculha Huracan. The second is Chip-Caculha. The third is Raxa-Caculha [all forms of lightning and thunder]. And these three are the Heart of Heaven.

Then Tepeu and Gucumatz came together; then they conferred about life and light, what they would do so that there would be light and dawn, who it would be who would provide food and sustenance.

Thus let it be done! Let the emptiness be filled! Let the water recede and make a void, let the earth appear and become solid; let it be done. Thus they spoke. Let there be light, let there be dawn in the sky and on the earth! There shall be neither glory nor grandeur in our creation and formation until the human being is made, man is formed. So they spoke.

Then the earth was created by them. So it was, in truth, that they created the earth. Earth! they said, and instantly it was made.

Like the mist, like a cloud, and like a cloud of dust was the creation, when the mountains appeared from the water; and instantly the mountains grew.

Only by a miracle, only by magic art were the mountains and valleys formed; and instantly the groves of cypresses and pines put forth shoots together on the surface of the earth.

And thus Gucumatz was filled with joy, and exclaimed: "Your coming has been fruitful, Heart of Heaven; and you, Huracan, and you, Chipi-Caculha, Raxa-Caculha!"

"Our work, our creation shall be finished," they answered.

First the earth was formed, the mountains and the valleys; the currents of water were divided, the rivulets were running freely between the hills, and the water was separated when the high mountains appeared.

Thus was the earth created, when it was formed by the Heart of Heaven, the Heart of Earth, as they are called who first made it fruitful, when the sky was in suspense, and the earth was submerged in the water.

So it was that they made perfect the work, when they did it after thinking and meditating upon it ...

Mayan people (Central America)

A Story of Our Times

In the middle of nowhere we saw a team of workmen dig something up. A few days later, we saw an earth-mover. A week later, a road. Three weeks later we saw a strip of tarmac. We knew then that Nomakhwezi had got herself a man with power. We knew he must be a minister. On a Sunday we saw a chauffeured black limousine cruising on the tarmac. It was the minister of finance.

Six weeks later we saw the same team of workers, digging,

chanting. A week later the tarmac was gone. We knew then there was either a *coup* or the affair was over. Seeing Khwezi at the bus stop was enough to tell us.

A month later we saw the same team of workers. We knew the lovers had made up. We organized a demonstration. Placards flew: 'Don't waste public funds', 'Down with . . .'

The workers organized a counter-demonstration. They accused us of taking their jobs from them. The lovers agreed.

Pitika Ntuli (Azania)

Dog Digs to China

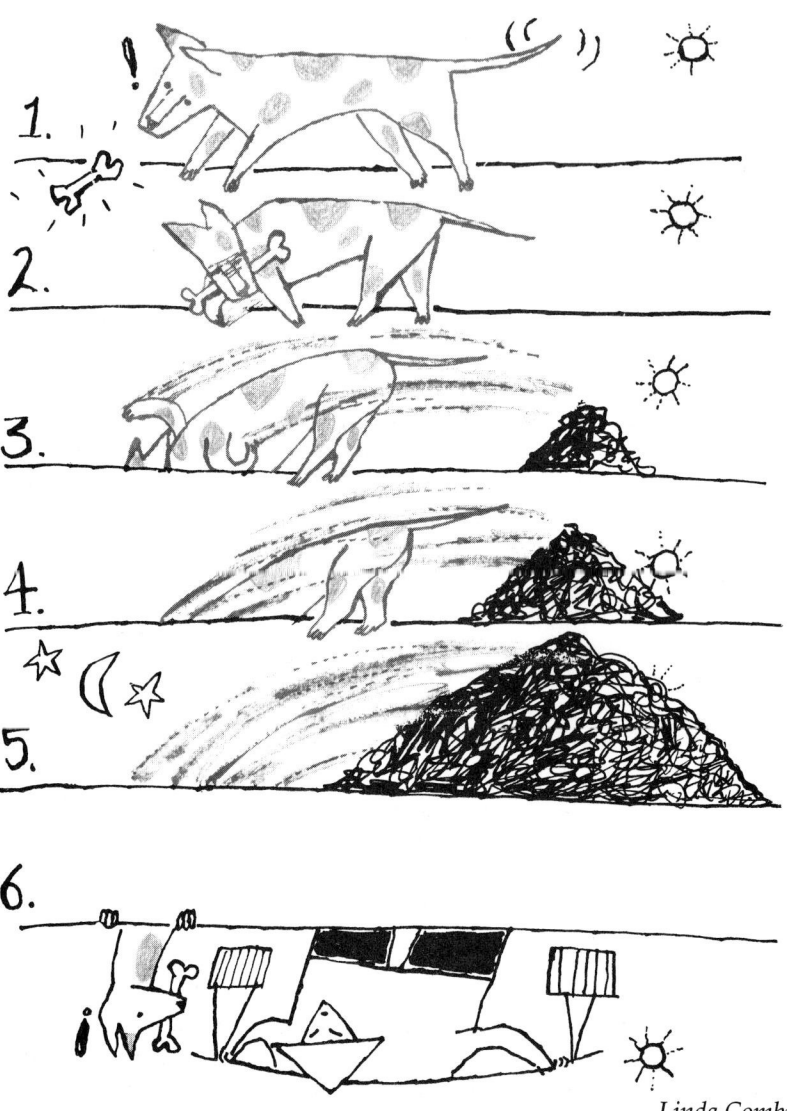

Linda Combi

The North Wind and the Sun

One morning the North Wind and the Sun saw a horseman wearing a new cloak.

"That young man looks very pleased with his new cloak," said the North Wind, "but I could easily blow it off his back if I wanted to."

"I don't think you could," said the Sun, "but let us both try to do it. You first."

The North Wind began to blow. People had to chase after their hats. Leaves were blown from the trees. All the animals were frightened. The ships in the harbour were sunk.

The North Wind blew with all his might, but it was no use, for the horseman just pulled his cloak more tightly around him.

"My turn now," said the Sun. And as he gave out his gentle heat, insects hummed and flowers opened. The birds began to sing. The animals lay down to sleep. People came out to gossip.

The horseman began to feel very hot, and when he came to a river he took off his clothes and went in for a swim.

So the Sun was able to achieve by warmth and gentleness what the North Wind in all his strength and fury could not do.

La Fontaine

The Chicks' Nest

The fledgelings were chirping away merrily in the foliage. At the foot of the tree, the bear cub looked all around him but couldn't see a bird's nest anywhere, which meant that he couldn't catch them, which left him hopping up and down with frustration.

"Why waste all that energy?" said the big black bear languidly, seeing the bear cub running around in circles. "You'll see the nest when the leaves fall in winter, and the chicks will be yours for the taking."

Winter came, and the leaves fell, and sure enough, there in the branches, all alone, was a nest.

"Oh! Where are the chirping chicks?" said the bear cub in wide-eyed wonder.

"They've flown south," the tree told him.

"Gone without a trace," the wind told him.

Wu Guangxiao

The Two Clay Men

Two clay men, one big one and one small one, stood warming themselves side by side on a table above a fiercely burning brazier. The big one waited till the little one was off his guard and shouldered him down into the brazier, leaving himself sole occupant of the table. Next morning when their owner came to clean the table and light the fire, he found the fallen clay man whole and unharmed. "So," he cried appreciatively, "the more you heat them, the sturdier and better looking they get!" And he put him back where he belonged.

If I'd known that, thought the big clay man, I'd have jumped in myself! This made him even more envious of the little clay man, and he waited till their owner was out and pushed him into the water tub, regaining sovereignty of the table.

Thanks to having been made hollow, and now having been fired, the little clay man neither sank nor dissolved; in fact he looked even more attractive wet. The big clay man took one look and was furious. He's not going to get away with showing off in front of the master, he thought, and with a flying leap he plunged into the water tub.

The owner looked high and low when he found them missing. He came across the little one first in the water tub, fished him out and carefully replaced him on the table and then looked for the big one. He couldn't find him anywhere, until after quite some time he noticed, right in the bottom of the water tub, a handful of powdered clay.

Du Li

Two Feminist Tales

The Giantess

Thousands of years ago in far away India, which is so far away that anything is possible, before the advent of the inevitable Aryans, a giantess was in charge of a little kingdom. It was small by her standards, but perhaps not by our own. Three oceans converged on its triangular tip, and in the north there were mountains, the tallest in the world, which would perhaps account for this singular kingdom. It was not a kingdom, but the word has been lost and I could find no other. There wasn't any king. The giantess governed and there were no other women. The men were innocent and happy and carefree. If they were hurt, they were quickly consoled. For the giantess was kind, and would set them on her knee and tell them they were brave and strong and noble. And if they were hungry, the giantess would feed them. The milk from her breasts was sweeter than honey and more nutritious than mangoes. If they grew fractious, the giantess would sing, and they would clamber up her leg and onto her lap and sleep unruffled. They were a happy people and things might have gone on in this way forever, were it not for the fact that the giantess grew tired. Her knees felt more bony, her voice rasped, and on one or two occasions she showed irritation. They were greatly distressed. "We love you," they said to the tired giantess, "Why won't you sing? Are you angry with us? What have we done?" "You are dear little children," the giantess replied, "but I have grown very tired and it's time for me to go." "Don't you love us anymore? We'll do what you want. We will make you happy. Only please don't go." "Do you know what I want?" the giantess asked. They were silent for a bit, then one of them said, "We'll make you our queen." And another one said, "We'll write you a poem." And the third one shouted (while turning cartwheels), "We'll bring you many gifts of oysters and pearls and pebbles and stones." "No," said the giantess, "No." She turned her back and crossed the mountains.

Of Cats and Bells

"Who will bell the cat?" "Not I," said the Brown Mouse, "I have too many babies, and a hundred things to do, and a long shopping list." "Not I," said the Blue Mouse, "I hate silly fights and I believe in peace." "Not I," said the Little Mouse, "I am too little, and the bell is too heavy." "Nor I," said the Big Mouse, "I do not understand the nature of bells, and moreover, they bore me." "Well, I'll bell the cat," said the Lunatic Mouse, "I'll do it for a lark. It's really quite funny." "No, I'll bell the cat," said the Heroic Mouse, "I want the glory." "If we wait long enough," said the Clever Mouse, "the cat will die, and then we needn't worry." "Yes," said the mice, "let us forget it;" and some didn't and some did.

Suniti Namjoshi

Anecdotes of Mr Keuner

Good Turns

As an example of how to do friends a good turn Mr K obliged with the following story. Three young men came to an old Arab and said: "Our father has died. He has left us seventeen camels and stipulated in his will that the eldest should have half, the second a third and the youngest a ninth of the camels. Now we can't agree amongst ourselves on the division: you decide the matter." The Arab thought about it and said: "As I see it, you have one camel too few to share them out properly. I've only got one camel myself, but it's at your disposal. Take it and share them out and give me back only what's left over." They thanked him for this good turn, took the camel with them and then divided the eighteen camels in such a way that the eldest got half - that is, nine - the second a third - that is, six - and the youngest a ninth - that is, two - of the camels. To their amazement when they had each led their camels aside, there was one over. This they took back to their old friend with renewed thanks.

Mr K called this the right sort of good turn, since it demanded no special sacrifice.

Bertolt Brecht

The Woodcutter's Son

Once upon a time, many years ago, there was a woodcutter, who was well-known around the village for his accuracy in shot and his knowledge of the forest: catching deer and rabbit and what have you.

One day he was taken seriously ill, and the illness lasted and lasted and went on and on and on. Eventually the family became very, very poor. He couldn't go out to carve wood or cut wood for the fire, so they had to send his son out.

Now the son wasn't that well either. One day the woodcutter sent him out with a donkey; and his mother gave him some cheese and some brown bread and a little drop of wine. Off he set - as I said he wasn't very strong - and was cutting away little bits of wood as best he could. He got very very tired quickly. He sat down on a stump to eat his cheese and his bread and his wine. Then he heard footsteps behind him and he turned round and an old gentleman was standing there.

"Good morrow, young fellow."

"Good morrow, sir."

"It's a beautiful day, isn't it?"

"It is, sir," the boy said, "a wonderful day. Would you care to join me with my cheese and bread and drop of wine?"

"Oh, thank you kindly, sonny Jim," the old gent replied. "And what are you doing?"

"I'm the old woodcutter's son," he said, "and he's been very poorly this last year or so. Now I've had to come out and get the wood. But I'm not as strong as my father; I can't get very big lumps of wood."

"Never mind my boy," he said, "God knows who needs it most, and He will look after us all in His own time. I'll give you a hand for my bread."

"No thank you, sir. I'm only too pleased to talk to you. I don't need any help; the donkey cart is nearly full anyway."

So he went home and he put the wood in the shed. He went indoors, and his mother said to him,

"How did you get on today?"

"Well, I got as much wood as I could mother. Funny thing though: all the times I've been in the forest with Dad - hunting rabbit, looking after the pheasant and hunting deer - I've never seen anyone else in that particular part of the forest. But today I saw an old gentleman; he shared my bread and wine with me, and my cheese. He offered to give me a hand to do the work and I said "No thank you, I've nearly finished." But he was a kind gentleman - wished us all well."

His father said, "You should have let him work for us son."

"But he was old and he didn't look very strong. No stronger than I am and I'm not very strong."

"Yes my son, but there are some people that are very proud; they like to work and earn what they receive."

"All right Father," said the boy, "if I see him again and he asks if he can give me a hand, I'll let him - but I won't force him to."

So the next day he went out, and he saw the old man again. They were sitting down talking and the old man said,

"You're not a very big fellow for your age, are you?"

"No,'' he said, "we don't have any meat now because Daddy's ill. We used to go hunting, but I don't know how to hunt - I haven't been taught."

"Never mind my boy, you'll get by one of these days, you'll get by."

The boy went home, and saw his mother.

"Hello Mother. What have we got for dinner tonight?"

"Rabbit stew."

"Rabbit stew! How did we get a rabbit stew?"

"It's simple. I was in the garden and I saw this stone amongst the carrots and I threw it. I saw something tumble over. When I went to look, there laid a rabbit. I must have struck it on the back of the head with the stone by accident. Lucky," she said, "we've got rabbit stew for tea tonight."

"That's good Mother. And that should do Father good and all."

So they had their tea.

"Mum," he said, "can I have a glass of milk?"

"Yes," she said, "but go easy. I've made two cheeses today, and there isn't a lot of milk."

So he went to the churn to take the milk and the churn was full of milk!

"Mum," he cried, "how many cheeses did you make today?"

"Two."

"But you've got a churn of milk."

"Oh don't be silly, son," she said, "you can't have a churn of milk if you started with a churn of milk. You use half a churn of milk to make cheese, a quarter of a churn to make butter ... how can you have a full churn of milk?"

"Mother, there *is* a full churn of milk."

She went to look. There *was* a full churn of milk.

"I can't make it out," she said.

"It must be a miracle," he said.

He went to the cupboard.

"How many cheeses did you make, Mum?"

"I keep telling you, *two*."

"Were there two here yesterday?"

"No, there was no cheese yesterday."

"But there are four in the cupboard."

"You're pulling my leg again."

"Mother, come and look."

When she looked in the cupboard, she saw four cheeses there right enough. She had to touch each of them in turn to make sure they were really there. She said,

"Let's have a good look to see whatever else has happened. I'll go to the bread cupboard. Now I *know* I only made two brown loaves, because I only had raw wheat. Now two brown loaves is all that should be in the bread cupboard."

But when they opened the bread cupboard, lo and behold there were three brown loaves and three white loaves!

"White loaves!" she thought, "white loaves? Only the miller can afford to make white loaves, because he gets the finest flour. Well," she said, "this *is* something; this is something of a miracle."

Anyway they went to bed, and the next morning they got up and the first thing she did was go to the cheese cupboard: there were the four cheeses. She went to the bread cupboard: there were the three brown loaves and the three white loaves. She went to the churn and the churn was still full of milk.

So she gave the boy his wine and she gave him a jug of milk; she gave him some brown bread *and* some white bread - and some butter. Now this boy's mother was well-known for her butter-making. She could make beautiful butter. But, of course, she never had enough milk to make the butter that she wanted to make. When she did make butter, no one had tasted anything like it anywhere.

The boy went out to chop his wood and gather his wood, and he met the old man again.

"Good morrow, kind sir."

"Good morning, young lad," the old man said, "and what have we got today?"

"Well," he said, "you know I told you about not having any meat for a long while? Well Mum was cleaning the garden, she threw a stone and hit a rabbit on the head. And we had rabbit for dinner."

"Oh, that was jolly good."

"I'll tell you what," he said, "I saved a leg for you."

"Oh, that was very kind of you."

"And Mother made some bread, and she made some butter, and we had some milk over, so I brought some milk with the wine today. And white bread - now we don't have white bread normally, only the miller's rich enough to have white bread. We used to, when Daddy was the King's Forester, but he's so ill he can't be the King's Forester any more."

So they sat down, and they ate the bread.

The boy said, "Oh, Mum gave me some butter. Would you like to try some of my mother's butter? My mother makes the finest butter. Now I'm not boasting because she's my mother. She's noted for it. You ask anybody in the village: my mother makes the finest butter."

"I'll try some," said the old man. He did. "You are not telling a lie my boy. This is the finest butter I've tasted. It's really beautiful; its marvellous."

The boy put a bit on his brown bread. Being the kind-hearted boy that he was, he gave the white bread to the poor old man. And when he tasted the butter he thought,

"Well, I know my mother makes good butter, but she's never made butter as good as this. This is as the old gentleman says, it's marvellous."

They finished their meal, then carried on together chopping their wood. Because there were two of them, they could put a bit extra in the donkey cart. The boy found some wild oats and he gave them to the donkey.

The old man looked up. "How long have you been poor, then?" he asked.

"Oh, for years now, since Dad was taken ill. And as I say, it's a miracle we have white bread because Mother can't afford the flour. We've only got a few coppers in a tin that we save for special occasions - and there's only a few pennies in that - that I do know."

"A few pennies?"

"Yes, just a few pennies."

"I don't think that your Mummy's got just a few pennies. I think she's got a little bit of gold in there and all."

The boy laughed. "You are a very lovely man, and you must know a lot, but I don't think you're right there. I know you're wrong. There's no gold in my Mummy's box."

"You never know. Have a look now and again; funny things can happen."

So the boy went home and his mother asked him how he had got on.

"Oo," she said, "that's a beautiful stack of timber you've got today."

But when he went to open the shed to put the wood away, he couldn't get the wood into the shed. The shed was crammed full of wood! Big pieces of wood, cut in quarters, just like his father used to do.

So he thought, "I'll stack it outside." He stacked it outside and he put the donkey in his stall. Then he went to get the donkey's food, and when he looked in the donkey's bin, he saw it was full of oats - and there was always - *always* - just a scraping at the bottom. It was full of oats, the big bin was full of oats! So he gave the donkey a big bucket of oats and he went indoors. His father was sitting by the fire.

"How do you feel today, Father?"

"I'm fine. I had a walk around the cottage this afternoon, and I managed to bag another couple of rabbits. I'm getting better and stronger. I used my gun today: two rabbits I got today. But," he said, "your mother was telling me about the bread, the milk and the cheese."

"Yes. And I've got something else to tell you, Father. The woodshed's full of wood."

"The woodshed's full of wood?"

"Yes. It's not the wood that I could have put there. I'm not strong enough to put that much wood there. And the butter that Mother made yesterday - you know she makes good butter - it was marvellous butter Dad. I've never tasted butter like it."

"Yes," said his mother, "I know I make good butter, and my mother taught me, but this was something different."

All of a sudden there was a knock on the door. There was a gentleman standing there, in fine livery. And he said,

"Is this the home of the woodcutter?"

"Yes it is," said the boy who had answered the door, "do you wish to see my father? Come in." And he bid him welcome.

"It's not your father I want to see this time. I've come to see your mother," he said, "I want to have some of her butter."

"But how did you hear of the butter?"

"A little bird told me about the butter, and I want some."

"Well," said the mother, "there's just a small pat of butter here. I'm going to make some later on for tomorrow, but you're welcome to this." And with that she wrapped it up and gave it to the gentleman.

And he said, "There you are, my dear madam, there is a little bit of gold for you," and he gave her a small gold coin.

Then the little boy remembered what the old gentleman had said in the forest - 'A little bit of gold will come into the box.' "Mum," he said, "the old gentleman told me about that little bit of gold to go in your box."

She said, "What box?"

"The box on the shelf that you keep the coppers in. He told me that there would be gold to go in that box."

"Oh well," she said, "to please you and your gentleman, I'll put it in the box."

But when she went to reach the box down, she could hardly lift it. She put it on the table. "What's this?" she wondered. She was very, very nervous. In fact she was frightened to open it, because although it was a big box, it wasn't a heavy box, and she knew there were no more than four of five copper pennies in there.

But when she opened the top there it was: near to running over - not with pennies, but with gold coins - every one of them perfect and shiny. She called her husband and he stared at it.

He said, "We're rich, we're rich beyond compare. We must celebrate. We must find that old gentleman, because ever since our little son Thomas met him and spoke to him we've had nothing but good luck."

So the father and his son went into the forest, looking for the old gentleman. All of a sudden they heard a noise and they turned round and there was the King. The King and his huntsmen were standing there.

"Good morrow, woodcutter," said the King.

"Good morrow, your Royal Highness. I'm sorry your Royal Highness that I'm standing in your way."

"That's quite all right. Hello my young fellow, young Tommy, how are you?"

"I'm fine, your Majesty."

"And what are you doing in the forest?"

"I'm looking for a friend of mine."

"Looking for a friend?"

"Yes, your Majesty. A very old man used to come into the forest while my father was ill, and he used to share my food and help me cut wood. And he told me all kinds of funny stories: there'd be gold in my mother's copper box, there'd be plenty of wood for the winter, and we would have meat upon the table. And sure enough, what he said has come true. And I wish to meet the old man."

The King laughed. He called the woodcutter to his side, and whispered into his ear, and he said,

"Is that agreed then?"

"Yes, your Majesty. As from tomorrow I will regain my position as Chief Forester and Woodcutter to His Royal Highness." And with that they bid the King goodbye and walked home.

But the boy was still anxious because he hadn't met the old man. He was worried, and he couldn't sleep. He went to bed that night with just a little tear on his cheek - and eventually he did fall asleep.

He woke up next morning and he said, "Mother, mother, I must find that old man. I know why I didn't find him yesterday, because I was with Father. I think I've got to be on my own to see him."

And off he went with his donkey; he gathered some wild oats in the forest as he went along and fed them to his donkey. They came to the stump where he normally sat down to have his dinner, and he sat there. And he heard the voice:

"Good morrow, young lad."

"Good morrow, kind sir. I looked for you yesterday with my father. Thanks to you," he said, "my father is well. He's got his job back with the King. We've plenty of wood, plenty of butter, plenty of cheese and plenty of milk; and we've plenty of gold too, and my mother and father said we must celebrate. And you must celebrate with us. You must come to my house, and have a meal and celebrate."

"That I will this very day," said the old man.

And they went back to the boy's house and they had dinner. The boy asked the old man, "Why didn't you show yourself yesterday when I was with my father?"

"Ah, but I did. I did show myself yesterday, and I spoke to you yesterday."

"You couldn't have spoken to me yesterday. If you had spoken to me yesterday, surely I would have known."

"Well, you did speak with me yesterday, young lad," he said, "but you didn't know me, not sitting on my fine horse, with my fine gown and my fine golden crown upon my head."

"Your Majesty!"

"Yes, I am the King of this land. I heard of your father, and I heard of your mother's plight. But don't think it was all my doing.

Although I am a King, when I was a boy like you I used to go to the forest with my father. One day I got lost and I had my food the same as you did, and I fed a little old man - and when I say a little old man, I mean a *little* old man and he was a fairy; the King of the Fairies to be precise. He gave me a blessing that if I touched anybody's head after touching my crown, whatever I wished for them that night would come true. And I wished it on you, my son, because you are kind. Not many in my land are as kind as your father, your mother and you. Now, you will be made a Royal Page in the Royal Household, and your family will never want."

And they never did.

Fred Manley

Images towards Story-Writing

Linda Combi

THE VOICE ON THE PAGE

Timelines

Year	Age	Local/World Event (Historical)	Internal Discovery	External Event
1878	3			Moved to Botswana. Started in first school (play school).
1979	4	Mrs Thatcher came into power.	Began a different way of life.	Went to first primary school.
1980	5	Falklands War	Began to envy my older brother. Started copying everything he did.	Began to enjoy life in Botswana.
1981	6		Became a nuisance to the family at times.	
1982	7	Botswana's first president dies. (Sir Seretse Khama)	Began an image of general happiness.	
1983	8			I changed school and met new friends.
1984	9	S.A. Raids on its surrounding countries against A.N.C. (African National Congress)	Began to acknowledge S.A situation and became full of resentment.	
1985	10	Live Aid and Band Aid.	First acknowledgement of opposite sex. Major infatuation.	First girl friend.
1986	11	Americans bomb Libya Chernobyl.	Acknowledgement of world news and events.	First try of cigarette (disliked).
1987	12		Met more new friends and was very happy.	Preparation to leave Botswana (perhaps). New school.
1988	13	Seoul Olympics Lockerbie disaster Clapham disaster	Rather depressing start to life in England. First time boarding. (Very difficult). Sudden change of lifestyle.	First real girlfriend; Left Botswana for England.
1989	14	Mandela was freed. Tiananmen Square disaster. San Fransisco earthquake Hillsborough football disaster	Began to enjoy life in U.K much more.	My mother and brother joined us in U.K (during Christmas 88/89).
1990	15	Gulf Crisis Liberation of Eastern Europe. German unification World Cup. (W. Germany winners).	Forced to open my eyes to world affairs. Realised I was in love (although this was opposed by many factors).	First time in love. First holiday back in Botswana (long awaited).

Gabriel Swartland

Year	Age	Local/World Event (Historical)	Internal discovery	External event
1978	4		Developed temporary fear of water.	Nearly drowned; began school.
1979	5	Margaret Thatcher elected P.M.		Went to America, first time abroad.
1980	6	Falklands War.	Happy at school.	
1981	7		Become increasingly confident. Pride in new brother. Unsure of Steiner Education.	Changed school for the first time. Brother born.
1982	8			
1983	9		Very distressed about my grandmother's illness. Finding it hard to come to terms with.	Grandmother develops Alzheimers disease.
1984	10		Much happier in normal state education.	Changed school again.
1985	11	Third World Famine.	Unhappy on account of bullying.	Changed schools; began secondary education.
1986	12	American bombing of Libya; Chernobyl.	Confused emotions; experiencing fear of many things. Unhappy at school, great loss of confidence.	
1987	13		Moody and depressed. Much happier at school; developing interest in boys.	First boyfriend.
1988	14	Lockerbie air disaster. Zeebrugge ferry disaster.	Wanting more freedom.	First cigarette. First time drunk (seriously).
1989	15	Earthquakes in San Francisco. Tiananmen Square tragedy. Hillsborough football disaster.	Regaining some of my previous confidence.	Embarked on G.C.S.E.
1990	16	Gulf Crisis. German Unification.	Going through many changes. Learning about myself. Very happy but wanting more independence.	Did well in exams. First serious and physical relationship with an older man.

Amy Strickland

'Everyone thought he was cool and tough ...'

Everyone thought he was cool and tough, and he acted that way. He had feelings but they just died somewhere. He's only sixteen, and he feels nothing. He's like a zombie. People die and his friends die, and it doesn't affect him. He never cries and he never cares deeply for anyone. I just think it's a waste because I remember him before.

When he was young, when we were little kids in grade school, he was really sweet and he did care then and he had feelings. It's just sad to watch him over the years, to regress like that and lose his feelings. When people hurt my feelings, I get it over with. I don't turn bitter. He turned bitter and cynical. He just takes everything as a personal offense. It all accumulates and he can't talk about it so he turns inward.

He's seventeen now and he's in jail. So that's about it. He was my buddy for about four years. But then we went our separate ways. I don't know where he is. I did last year but there was nothing left to say. It wasn't the same any more. He's a human being, he's intelligent and now he's a drug addict, sitting in jail. He's wasted.

He was a good little kid, nice and funny. He was everybody's boy, the little boy you'd like to have for your son. That was him. Mr Nice Little Boy. (Laughs.) He had talent. I think he would have been an artist. He was always drawing and did good work. He had imagination. When he was seven or eight, he would draw purple cows. Everybody would say: "What are you drawing purple cows for?" He'd say: "Purple cows are pretty. When I'm older, I'll be a farmer and I'll breed purple cows." He was really wild that way. He started hanging around with the older gang members - you know, a tough gang member doesn't stand around with a paintbrush, drawing. Not in my neighborhood. So he gave it up.

Now everyone in the neighborhood is afraid of him. If he wasn't in jail, if he was walking down the street, everybody would go in their houses. He wouldn't do anything to them, but that's the way they feel because they've heard of him now. He's created this image for himself, and now he's stuck with it.

In the sixties is when the gangs started getting prominent in my neighborhood. They'd beat you up every day until you finally agreed to join them. He was so young, he didn't know what he was getting into. They were always beating him up, so he figured: Okay, I'll join. The girl members are as mean as the guys. (Laughs.)

They don't mind me. We still get along. We kind of accept each other. I'm about one of five people in the neighborhood that they'll associate with that are not in their gangs. They don't try. They think I'm silly for not joining, and I think they're silly. But we get along.

My other friends think they're low-down scum. They can't see how I would even say hello to them on the street. They think it's unusual that I'm able to talk to them yet.

I always aggravate my dad because I'm always trying to see the good in everybody. There's a few I can't tolerate but most of 'em I get along with.

Linda Haas

The Projectile

We sipped tea. Politely musing
on possible reasons for the success
of my books in your country. Slipped
into talk of pain and humiliation
you find occurring, and reoccurring,
in my stories. And that element
of sheer chance. How all this translates
in terms of sales.
I looked into a corner of the room.
And for a minute I was 16 again,
careening around in the snow
in a '50 Dodge sedan with five or six
bozos. Giving the finger
to some other bozos, who yelled and pelted
our car with snowballs, gravel, old
tree branches. We spun away, shouting.
And we were going to leave it at that.
But my window was down three inches.
Only three inches. I hollered out
one last obscenity. And saw this guy
wind up to throw. From this vantage, now,
I imagine I see it coming. See it
speeding through the air while I watch,
like those soldiers in the first part
of the last century watched canisters
of shot fly in their direction
while they stood, unable to move
for the dread fascination of it.
But I *didn't* see it. I'd already turned
my head to laugh with my pals.
When something slammed into the side
of my head so hard it broke my eardrum and fell
in my lap, intact. A ball of packed ice
and snow. The pain was stupendous.
And the humiliation.
It was awful when I began to weep
in front of those tough guys while they
cried, *Dumb luck. Freak accident.*
A chance in a million!

The guy who threw it, he had to be amazed
and proud of himself while he took
the shouts and backslaps of the others.
He must have wiped his hands on his pants.
And messed around a little more
before going home to supper. He grew up
to have his share of setbacks and got lost
in his life, same as I got lost in mine.
He never gave that afternoon
another thought. And why should he?
So much else to think about always.
Why remember that stupid car sliding
down the road, then turning the corner
and disappearing?
We politely raise our teacups in the room.
A room that for a minute something else entered.

Raymond Carver

Testament of a Little Doffer

What age are you?
Twenty-three.

Where do you live?
At Leeds.

What time did you begin work at the factory?
When I was six years old.

At whose factory did you work?
Mr Burk's.

What kind of mill is it?
Flax mill.

What was your business in that mill?
I was a little doffer.

What were your hours of labour in that mill?
From 5 in the morning till 9 at night, when they were thronged*.

For how long a time together have you worked that excessive length of time?
For about a year.

What were the usual hours of labour when you were not so thronged?
From six in the morning till seven at night.

What time was allowed for meals?
Forty minutes at noon.

* thronged: *busy*

Had you any time to get your breakfast or drinking?
No, we had to get it as we could.

Do you consider doffing a laborious employment?
Yes.

Explain what you had to do?
When the frames are full, they have to stop the frames and take the flyers off, and take the full bobbins off, and carry them to the rollers, and then put empty ones on, and set the frame going again.

Does that keep you constantly on your feet?
Yes, there are so many frames and they run so quick.

Your labour is very excessive?
Yes, you have not time for anything.

Suppose you flagged a little, or were late, what would they do?
Strap us.

And they are in the habit of strapping those who are last in doffing?
Yes.

Constantly?
Yes.

Girls as well as boys?
Yes.

Have you ever been strapped?
Yes.

Severely?
Yes.

Is the strap used so as to hurt you excessively?
Yes, it is ... I have seen the overlooker go to the top end of the room, where the little girls hug the can to the backminders; he has taken a strap, and a whistle in his mouth, and sometimes he has got a chain and chained them, and strapped them all down the room.

What was his reason for that?
He was very angry.

Did you live far from the mill?
Yes, two miles.

Had you a clock?
No, we had not.

Were you generally there in time?
Yes, my mother has been up at 4 o'clock in the morning, and at 2 o'clock in the morning; the colliers used to go to their work at 3 or 4 o'clock, and when she heard them stirring she has got up out of her warm bed, and gone out and asked them the time; and I have

sometimes been at Hunslet Carr at 2 o'clock in the morning, when it was streaming down with rain, and we have had to stay till the mill was opened.

You are considerably deformed in person as a consequence of this labour?
Yes I am.

And what time did it come on?
I was about 13 years old when it began coming, and it has got worse since; it is five years since my mother died, and my mother was never able to get me a good pair of stays to hold me up, and when my mother died I had to do for myself, and got me a pair.

Were you perfectly straight and healthy before you worked at a mill?
Yes, I was as straight a little girl as ever went up and down town.

Were you straight till you were 13?
Yes I was.

Did your deformity come upon you with much pain and weariness?
Yes, I cannot express the pain all the time it was coming.

Do you know of anybody that has been similarly injured in their health?
Yes, in their health, but not many deformed as I am.

It is very common to have weak ankles and crooked knees?
Yes, very common indeed.

This is brought on by stopping the spindle?
Yes.

Where are you now?
In the poorhouse.

State what you think as to the circumstances in which you been placed during all this time of labour, and what you have considered about it as to the hardship and cruelty of it?

The witness was too much affected to answer the question.

Evidence of a Female Millhand to the Parliamentary Commissioners, 1815

Elizabeth Bentley

'I have to be a waitress ...'

I have to be a waitress. How else can I learn about people? How else does the world come to me? I can't go to everyone. So they have to come to me. Everyone wants to eat, everyone has hunger. And I serve them. If they've had a bad day, I nurse them, cajole them.

Maybe with coffee I give them a little philosophy. They have cocktails, I give them political science.

I'll say things that bug me. If they manufacture soap, I say what I think about pollution. If it's automobiles, I say what I think about them. If I pour water I say, "Would you like your quota of mercury today?" If I serve cream, I say, "Here is your substitute. I think you're drinking plastic." I just can't keep quiet. I have an opinion on every single subject there is. In the beginning it was theology, and my bosses didn't like it. Now I am a political and my bosses don't like it. I speak *sotto voce*. But if I get heated, then I don't give a damn. I speak like an Italian speaks. I can't be servile. I give service. There is a difference.

I'm called by my first name. I like my name. I hate to be called Miss. Even when I serve a lady, a strange woman, I will not say madam. I hate ma'am. I always say milady. In the American language there is no word to address a woman, to indicate whether she's married or unmarried. So I say milady. And sometime I playfully say to the man milord.

It would be very tiring if I had to say, "Would you like a cocktail?" and say that over and over. So I come out different for my own enjoyment. I would say, "What's exciting at the bar that I can offer?" I can't say, "Do you want coffee?" Maybe I'll say, "Are you in the mood for coffee?" Or, "The coffee sounds exciting." Just rephrase it enough to make it interesting for me. That would make them take an interest. It becomes theatrical and I feel like Mata Hari and it intoxicates me.

People imagine a waitress couldn't possibly think or have any kind of aspiration other than to serve food. When somebody says to me, "You're great, how come you're *just* a waitress?" *Just* a waitress. I'd say, "Why, don't you think you deserve to be served by me?" It's implying that he's not worthy, not that I'm not worthy. It makes me irate. I don't feel lowly at all. I myself feel sure. I don't want to change the job. I love it.

Tips? I feel like Carmen. It's like a gypsy holding out a tambourine and they throw the coin. (Laughs.) If you like people, you're not thinking of the tips. I never count my money at night. I always wait till morning. If I thought about my tips I'd be uptight. I never look at a tip. You pick it up fast. I would do my bookkeeping in the morning. It would be very dull for me to know I was making so much and no more. I do like challenge. And it isn't demeaning, not for me. ...

Postscript: *"After sixteen years - that was seven years ago - I took a trip to Hawaii and the Caribbean for two weeks. Went with a lover. The kids saw it - they're all married now. (Laughs.) One of my daughters said, "Act your age." I said, "Honey, if I were acting my age, I wouldn't be walking. My bones would ache. You don't want to hear about my arthritis. Aren't you glad I'm happy?"*

Dolores Dante

Family Snaps

John

I was born in 1925 in the island of Barbados, in a village called Durham. We moved to Josey Hill where my father bought a bungalow when I was eight.

My father was an engineer, responsible for men building roads and bridges, and for a quarry and all the equipment and explosives. He died in 1950, aged 67. My mother is the greatest, a pastor in a Pentecostal church who really believes in living what she preaches. They were a great couple. My dad held his head high in truth, my mother preached, and all the family was involved.

I was one of six brothers. We used to be called 'the Best brothers' or the 'Best boys' (Best is John's surname) and that was the truth. We never said "that's mine" or "that's his" but "that's ours". Although two of my brothers were six-footers and I am only five-foot-six, we never knew whose trousers we were wearing until one of us would find the legs either miles too long or miles too short. We were a close-knit family.

There was this sort of family-friendly relationship which meant that you knew what other people were feeling. Not just your parents, but beyond them into the village. You didn't have to ask people "What do you want?" or "Why didn't you come?" because you'd already know the answers, you'd know what was building up all the time.

When I look back, I see myself learning very very quick. I knew how my mother felt and I wouldn't want to play her up more than I had to, and I would be very angry with anyone else who did. If I played up some other woman, I'd know she feels it like my mother does. It didn't take me long to realise that.

My mother's main rule for us was that you had to go to Sunday School until you left primary school. She felt you had to serve Christ this way, and it gave you that extra little bit of reading practice. My mother is one of the fastest readers I've ever seen, and I'm not talking about the Bible because she doesn't need to read that - ask her a passage, and she'll give it word for word from her head. She was so fluent, and so were my brothers, that it's no wonder I'm still trying to grasp a little bit of education.

Perhaps I have passed it on. Everyone of my children went to Sunday School. Then they started to grow up and think "I don't want this," and I don't want to make them. I still believe, but I begin to wonder a lot more now.

If I can go back to a dream, a silly little dream. I dreamt one night, when I must have been about seven, that a sparrow came to me and said "Eat sugar, because if you don't eat sugar you're going to die." And I was scared, and I started to scream. The old lady got hold of me and put me to kneel down, and started to pray over me. I was scared and something got hold of me. I used to think "What's going to happen to me, looking round corners, getting visions of what's going to happen?" Slowly but surely, things that were going to happen started to come to me, and slowly I started to tell my mother things that were coming into my mind. She would make a note of them, and these things started to materialise. She said to me "Be careful, when something comes to you, think about it, don't brush it aside. Think in details and see what shape it takes."

Up to now this still happens. I'm wondering what it really is. Some part of the mind that doesn't take shape in certain people as it does in others? It's asleep in other people, this part. There's something causes it to wake up in some, and I believe this little dream did that with me.

I went on my apprenticeship the same year my brother died, and I had been on it a couple of weeks when he got killed. I was at the factory that night and somebody came and told the manager. But they never told me. The manager was on what they called 'the walk' above the wheels and rollers where the cane is being ground and the juice made into sugar and syrup and what-have-you. I was up there too, watching to see what was happening below. And this chap came in exhausted and said Evelyn had been hit at the top of Chancel Hill. When he said this I just left. I heard a shout "Hey, you come back" and I knew it was the manager, but I just kept going.

I can remember I ran out of the factory. I didn't take the highway, I went through what they called the back-alley of the trees, about a quarter of a mile of woodland. It was very dark, because the trees met overhead and entwined. I ran straight to the bottom of Chancel Hill, and I flog my way up to the top. When I got to my brother, he was lay there, and he was groaning and saying "I'm burning up inside, I want a drink of water." I went to him, and I said "Evelyn" and he said "John, at last you're here." He patted me on the back and said "It's been an accident . . . I want a drink of water." So I asked someone to get some water and gave him a drink, and he said "Oh, that's a whole lot better. " And I said "Isn't it ridiculous what happened?" He says to me "Well, don't cry. Don't be afraid, because I'll always be with you." And that was it. He died with his head on my knee.

John Best

'I used to think babies ...'

I used to think babies came from Palmolive soap. You see, mum only had perfumed soap in the house when the midwife was coming round to deliver the baby. She used to go all posh then and buy the soap and we were so innocent, not knowing how babies were conceived, we thought you made them from Palmolive soap. I was about thirteen at the time, and I used to go round saying to me friends, "If you want a baby, get some Palmolive soap." Anyway, when I was about sixteen dad used to do his nut about staying out late. If you arrived in late after the dance, he'd be waiting at the bottom of the road, take my dance shoes from me and flip me all the way back home with them. About this time I was having a lot of trouble with my periods and mum took me to the doctor's. Well, after examining me, he asked me what I thought was a very stupid question. Had I been naughty? I was flabbergasted. What on earth was that to do with the pain I'd been having? Well, I looked at mum, found she was blushing to the collar and I thought I'd better own up. Yes, I had been, actually. I'd broken a cup the previous day. That doctor nearly went into hysterics. He eventually took my mother aside and whispered a few words. And when we got outside I exploded to mum about the silly doctor, to ask such a stupid question. She didn't answer, just told me to hurry up as we had to get dad's tea. She didn't tell us anything about sex, and what we heard in the factory we didn't believe anyway. It was talked and laughed about in a very crude way and I just couldn't believe it, because for the life of me I couldn't imagine our vicar doing those sort of things. Why he kept coming to mind then I don't know - probably because he was the most respected person I knew.

Iris Bradford

The Toilet

Sometimes I wanted to give up and be a good girl who listened to her elders. Maybe I should have done something like teaching or nursing as my mother wished. People thought these professions were respectable, but I knew I wanted to do something different, though I was not sure what. I thought a lot about acting. My mother said that it had been a waste of good money educating me because I did not know what to do with the knowledge I had acquired. I'd come to Johannesburg for the December holidays after writing my matric exams, and then stayed on, hoping to find something to do.

My elder sister worked in Orange Grove as a domestic worker, and I stayed with her in her back room. I didn't know anybody in Jo'burg except my sister's friends whom we went to church with. The Methodist church up Fourteenth Avenue was about the only outing we had together. I was very bored and lonely.

On weekdays I was locked in my sister's room so that the Madam wouldn't see me. She was at home most of the time: painting her nails, having tea with her friends, or lying in the sun by the swimming pool. The swimming pool was very close to the room, which is why I had to keep very quiet. My sister felt bad about locking me in there, but she had no alternative. I couldn't even play the radio, so she brought me books, old magazines, and newspapers from the white people. I just read every single thing I came across: *Fair Lady*, *Woman's Weekly*, anything. But then my sister thought I was reading too much.

"What kind of wife will you make if you can't even make baby clothes, or knit yourself a jersey? I suppose you will marry an educated man like yourself, who won't mind going to bed with a book and an empty stomach."

We would play cards at night when she knocked off, and listen to the radio, singing along softly with the songs we liked. Then I got this temporary job in a clothing factory in town. I looked forward to meeting new people, and liked the idea of being out of the room for a change. The factory made clothes for ladies' boutiques.

The whole place was full of machines of all kinds. Some people were sewing, others were ironing with big heavy irons that pressed with a lot of steam. I had to cut all the loose threads that hang after a dress or a jacket is finished. As soon as a number of dresses in a certain style were finished, they would be sent to me and I had to count them, write the number down, and then start with the cutting of the threads. I was fascinated to discover that one person made only sleeves, another the collars, and so on until the last lady put all the pieces together, sewed on buttons, or whatever was necessary to finish.

Most people at the factory spoke Sotho, but they were nice to me - they tried to speak to me in Zulu or Xhosa, and they gave me all kinds of advice on things I didn't know. There was this girl, Gwendolene - she thought I was very stupid - she called me a 'bari' because I always sat inside the changing room with something to read when it was time to eat my lunch, instead of going outside to meet guys. She told me it was cheaper to get myself a 'lunch boy' - somebody to buy me lunch. She told me it was wise not to sleep with him, because then I could dump him anytime I wanted to. I was very nervous about such things. I thought it was better to be a 'bari' than to be stabbed by a city boy for his money.

The factory knocked off at four-thirty, and then I went to a park near where my sister worked. I waited there till half past six, when I could sneak into the house again without the white people seeing me. I had to leave the house before half past five in the mornings as well. That meant I had to find something to do with the time I had before I could catch the seven-thirty bus to work - about two hours. I would go to a public toilet in the park. For some reason it was never locked, so I would go in and sit on the toilet seat to read some magazine or other until the right time to catch the bus.

The first time I went into this toilet, I was on my way to the bus stop. Usually I went to the bus stop outside the OK Bazaars where it was well lit, and I could see. I would wait there, reading, or just looking at the growing number of cars and buses on the way to town. On this day it was raining quite hard, so I thought I would shelter in the toilet until the rain had passed. I knocked first to see if there was anyone inside. As there was no reply, I pushed the door open and went in. It smelled a little - a dryish kind of smell, as if the toilet was not used all that often, but it was quite clean compared to many 'Non-European' toilets I knew. The floor was painted red and the walls were cream white. It did not look like it had been painted for a few years. I stood looking around, with the rain coming very hard on the zinc roof. The noise was comforting - to know I had escaped the wet - only a few of the heavy drops had got me. The plastic bag in which I carried my book and purse and neatly folded pink handkerchief was a little damp, but that was because I had used it to cover my head when I ran to the toilet. I pulled my dress down so it would not get creased when I sat down. The closed lid of the toilet was going to be my seat for many mornings after that.

 I was really lucky to have found that toilet because the winter was very cold. Not that it was any warmer in there, but once I'd closed the door it used to be a little less windy. Also the toilet was very small - the walls were wonderfully close to me. It felt like it was made to fit me alone. I enjoyed that kind of privacy. I did a lot of thinking while I sat on that toilet seat. I did a lot of daydreaming too - many times imagining myself in some big hall doing a really popular play with other young actors. At school we took set books like *Buzani KuBawo* or *A Man For All Seasons* and made school plays which we toured to the other schools on weekends. I loved it very much. When I was even younger I had done little sketches taken from the Bible and on big days like Good Friday, we acted and sang happily.

 I would sit there dreaming ...

 I was getting bored with the books I was reading - the love stories all sounded the same, and besides that I just lost interest. I started asking myself why I had not written anything since I left school. At least at school I had written some poems, or stories for the school magazine, school competitions and other magazines like *Bona* and *Inkqubela*. Our English teacher was always so encouraging; I remembered the day I showed him my first poem - I was so excited I couldn't concentrate in class for the whole day. I didn't know anything about publishing then, and I didn't ask myself if my stories were good enough. I just enjoyed writing things down when I had the time. So one Friday, after I'd started being that toilet's best customer, I bought myself a notebook in which I hoped to write something. I didn't use it for quite a while, until one evening.

 My sister had taken her usual Thursday afternoon off, and she had delayed somewhere. I came back from work, then waited in the park for the right time to go back into the yard. The white people always had their supper at six-thirty and that was the time I used to steal my way in without disturbing them or being seen. My comings and goings had to be secret because they still didn't know I stayed there.

 Then I realised that she hadn't come back, and I was scared to go out again, in case something went wrong this time. I decided to sit down in front of my sister's room, where I thought I wouldn't be noticed. I was reading a copy of *Drum Magazine* and hoping that she would come back soon - before the dogs sniffed me out. For the first time I realised how stupid it was of me not to have cut myself a spare key long ago. I kept on hearing noises that sounded like the gate opening. A few times I was sure I had heard her footsteps on the concrete steps leading to the servant's quarters, but it turned out to be something or someone else.

I was trying hard to concentrate on my reading again, when I heard the two dogs playing, chasing each other nearer and nearer to where I was sitting. And then, there they were in front of me, looking as surprised as I was. For a brief moment we stared at each other, then they started to bark at me. I was sure they would tear me to pieces if I moved just one finger, so I sat very still, trying not to look at them, while my heart pounded and my mouth went dry as paper.

They barked even louder when the dogs from next door joined in, glared at me through the openings in the hedge. Then the Madam's high-pitched voice rang out above the dogs barking.

"Ireeeeeeeene!" That's my sister's English name, which we never use. I couldn't move or answer the call - the dogs were standing right in front of me, their teeth so threateningly long. When there was no reply, she came to see what was going on.

"Oh, it's you? Hello." She was smiling at me, chewing that gum which never left her mouth, instead of calling the dogs away from me. They had stopped barking, but they hadn't moved - they were still growling at me, waiting for her to tell them what to do.

"Please Madam, the dogs will bite me," I pleaded, not moving my eyes from them.

"No, they won't bite you." Then she spoke to them nicely, "Get away now - go on," and they went off. She was like a doll, her hair almost orange in colour, all curls round her made-up face. Her eyelashes fluttered like a doll's. Her thin lips were bright red like her long nails, and she wore very high-heeled shoes. She was still smiling; I wondered if it didn't hurt after a while. When her friends came for a swim, I could always hear her forever laughing at something or other.

She scared me - I couldn't understand how she could smile like that but not want me to stay in her house.

"When did you come in? We didn't see you."

"I've been here for some time now - my sister isn't here. I'm waiting to talk to her."

"Oh - she's not here?" She was laughing, for no reason that I could see. "I can give her a message - you go on home - I'll tell her that you want to see her."

Once I was outside the gate, I didn't know what to do or where to go. I walked slowly, kicking my heels. The street lights were so very bright! Like big eyes staring at me. I wondered what the people who saw me thought I was doing, walking around at that time of the night. But then I didn't really care, because there wasn't much I could do about the situation right then. I was just thinking how things had to go wrong on that day particularly, because my sister and I were not on such good terms. Early that morning, when the alarm had gone for me to wake up, I did not jump to turn it off, so my sister got really angry with me. She had gone on about me always leaving it to ring for too long, as if it was set for her, and not for me. And when I went out to wash, I had left the door open a second too long, and that was enough to earn me another scolding.

Every morning I had to wake up straight away, roll my bedding and put it all under the bed where my sister was sleeping. I was not supposed to put on the light although it was still dark. I'd light a candle, and tiptoe my way out with a soap dish and a toothbrush. My clothes were on a hanger on a nail at the back of the door. I'd take the hanger and close the door as quietly as I could. Everything had to be ready set the night before. A washing basin full of cold water was also ready outside the door, put there because the sound of running water and the loud screech the taps made in the morning could wake the white people and they would wonder what my sister was doing up so early. I'd do my everything and be off the premises by five-thirty with my shoes in my bag. I only put them on once I was safely out of the gate. And that gate made such a noise too. Many times I wished I could jump over it and save all that sickening careful-careful business!

Thinking about all these things took my mind away from the biting cold of the night and my wet nose, until I saw my sister walking towards me.

"Mholo, what are you doing outside in the street?" she greeted me. I quickly briefed her on what had happened.

"Oh Yehovah! You can be so dumb sometimes! What were you doing inside in the first place? You know you should have waited for me so we could walk in together. Then I could say you were visiting me or something. Now, you tell me, what I'm supposed to say to them if they see you come in again? Hayil." She walked angrily towards the gate, with me hesitantly following her. When she opened the gate, she turned to me with an impatient whisper.

"And now, why don't you come in, stupid?" I mumbled my apologies and followed her in. By some miracle no one seemed to have noticed us, and we quickly munched a snack of cold chicken and boiled potatoes and drank our tea, hardly on speaking terms. I just wanted to howl like a dog. I wished somebody would come and be my friend, and tell me that I was not useless, and that my sister did not hate me, and tell me that one day, I would have a nice place to live ... anything. It would have been really great to have someone my own age to talk to.

But also I knew that my sister was worried for me, she was scared of her employers. If they were to find out that I lived with her, they would fire her, and then we would both be walking up and down the streets. My eleven rand wasn't going to help us at all. I don't know how long I lay like that, unable to fall asleep, just wishing and wishing with tears running into my ears.

The next morning I woke up long before the alarm went off, but I lay there feeling tired and depressed. If there was a way out, I would not have gone to work, but there was this other strong feeling or longing inside me. It was some kind of pain that pushed me to do everything at double speed and run to my toilet. I call it my toilet because that is exactly how I felt about it. It was very rare that I ever saw anybody else go in there in the mornings. It was like they all knew I was using it, and they had to lay off or something. When I went there, I didn't really expect to find it occupied.

I felt my spirits really lifting as I put on my shoes outside the gate. I made sure that my notebook was in my bag. In my haste I even forgot my lunchbox, but it didn't matter I was walking faster and my feet were feeling lighter all the time. Then I noticed that the door had been painted, and that a new window pane had replaced the old broken one. I smiled to myself as I reached the door. Before long I was sitting on that toilet seat, writing a poem.

Many more mornings saw me sitting there writing. Sometimes it did not need to be a poem; I wrote anything that came into my head - in the same way I would have done if I'd had a friend to talk to. I remember some days when I felt like I was hiding something from my sister. She did not know about my toilet in the park, and she was not in the least interested in my notebook.

Then one morning I wanted to write a story about what had happened at work the day before; the supervisor screaming at me for not calling her when I'd seen the people who stole two dresses at lunchtime. I had found it really funny. I had to write about it and I just hoped there were enough pages left in my notebook. It all came back to me, and I was smiling when I reached the door, but it wouldn't open. It was locked.

I think for the first time I accepted that the toilet was not mine after all ... Slowly I walked over to a bench nearby, watched the early spring sun come up, and wrote my story anyway.

Gcina Mhlope

A Recollection

My father's friend came once to tea.
He laughed and talked. He spoke to me.
But in another week they said
That friendly pink-faced man was dead.

"How sad . . ." they said, "the best of men ..."
So I said too, "How sad"; but then
Deep in my heart I thought, with pride,
"I know a person who has died".

Frances Cornford

Blind Date
TWO SIDES TO EVERY STORY DEPT.

Next time one of the gang brags about a caper with the opposite sex, take it with a grain of salt. Try a grain of pepper if you like spicy stories! 'Cause you're hearing only one version. You'll see what we mean when you read both sides of this account of a

Blind Date

HER STORY...   **THE PHONE CALL**   HIS STORY...

When he started talking, there was no stopping him. I couldn't get a word in edgewise. Yakkity-yakkity-yak!

Boy, was it tough talking to her. She wouldn't say a word. I had to carry on the whole conversation myself!

THE ARRIVAL

When he came to pick me up, and I saw that ridiculous outfit he was wearing, I almost died of embarrassment.

Man, did I look cool. Real sharp. You should have seen the look on her face when she first came to the door!

CONTINUED NEXT PAGE

THE MOVIE

HER STORY...

The way he carried on at the movie was atrocious, bellowing like a jackass. I wanted to crawl into a hole!

HIS STORY...

What a stiff *she* turned out to be. The funniest movie I ever saw, and she sits there like it was a funeral!

THE "HAMBURGER HEAVEN"

All I wanted was a coke, but he insisted on ordering a whole meal for me. It was awful. I wasn't even hungry!

Was I burned! After she lets me order the most expensive dish on the menu, she don't even touch one bite!

PICTURES BY BOB CLARKE

THE FUTURE

Would I go out with him again? Are you kidding? Why, if I *never* see him, it'll be much too soon to suit me!

Me... call her up again? For what... to tell her what a square she is? Listen, one date with her was plenty!

Bob Clarke

Learning to Stalk Muskrats

Learning to stalk muskrats took me several years.

I've always known there were muskrats in the creek. Sometimes when I drove late at night my headlights' beam on the water would catch the broad lines of ripples made by a swimming muskrat, a bow wave, converging across the water at the raised dark vee of its head. I would stop the car and go out: nothing. They eat corn and tomatoes from my neighbors' gardens, too, by night, so that my neighbors were always telling me that the creek was full of them. Around here, people call them 'mushrats'; Thoreau called them 'Musquashes.' They are not of course rats at all (let alone squashes). They are more like diminutive beavers, and, like beavers, they exuded a scented oil from musk glands under the base of the tail - hence the name. I had read in several respectable sources that muskrats are so wary they are almost impossible to observe. One expert who made a full-time study of large populations, mainly by examining 'sign' and performing autopsies on corpses, said he often went for weeks at a time without seeing a single living muskrat.

One hot evening three years ago. I was standing more or less *in* a bush. I was stock-still, looking deep into Tinker Creek from a spot on the bank opposite the house, watching a group of bluegills stare and hang motionless near the bottom of a deep, sunlit pool. I was focused for depth. I had long since lost myself, lost the creek, the day, lost everything but still amber depth. All at once I couldn't see. And then I could: a young muskrat had appeared on top of the water, floating on its back. Its forelegs were folded languourously across its chest; the sun shone on its upturned belly. Its youthfulness and rodent grin, coupled with its ridiculous method of locomotion, which consisted of a lazy wag of the tail assisted by an occasional dabble of a webbed hind foot, made it an enchanting picture of decadence, dissipation, and summer sloth. I forgot all about the fish.

But in my surprise at having the light come on so suddenly, and at having my consciousness returned to me all at once and bearing an inverted muskrat, I must have moved and betrayed myself. The kit - for I know now it was just a young kit - righted itself so that only its head was visible above water, and swam downstream, away from me. I extricated myself from the bush and foolishly pursued it. It dove sleekly, reemerged, and glided for the opposite bank. I ran along the bankside brush, trying to keep it in sight. It kept casting an alarmed look over its shoulder at me. Once again it dove, under a floating mat of brush lodged in the bank, and disappeared. I never saw it again. (Nor have I ever, despite all the muskrats I have seen, again seen a muskrat floating on its back.) But I did not know muskrats then; I waited panting, and watched the shadowed bank. Now I know that I cannot outwait a muskrat who knows I am there. The most I can do is get 'there' quietly, while it is still in its hole, so that it never knows, and wait there until it emerges. But then all I knew was that I wanted to see more muskrats.

I began to look for them day and night. Sometimes I would see ripples suddenly start beating from the creek's side, but as I crouched to watch, the ripples would die. Now I know what this means, and have learned to stand perfectly still to make out the muskrat's small, pointed face hidden under overhanging bank vegetation, watching me. That summer I haunted the bridges, I walked up creeks and down, but no muskrats ever appeared. You must just have to be there, I thought. You must have to spend the rest of your life standing in bushes. It was a once-in-a-lifetime thing, and you've had your once.

Then one night I saw another, and my life changed. After that I knew where they were in numbers, and I knew when to look. It was late dusk; I was driving home from a visit with friends. Just on the off chance I parked quietly by the creek, walked out on the narrow bridge over the shallows, and looked upstream. Someday, I had been telling myself for weeks, someday a muskrat is going to swim right through that channel in the cattails, and I am going to see it. That is precisely what happened. I looked up into the channel for a muskrat, and there it came, swimming right toward me. Knock; seek; ask. It seemed to swim with a side-to-side sculling motion of its vertically flattened tail. It looked bigger than the upside-down muskrat, and its face more reddish. In its mouth it clasped a twig of tulip tree. One thing amazed me: it swam right down the middle of the creek. I thought it would hide in the brush along the edge; instead, it plied the waters as obviously as an aquaplane. I could just look and look.

But I was standing on the bridge, not sitting, and it saw me. It changed its course, veered towards the bank, and disappeared behind an indentation in the rushy shoreline. I felt a rush of such pure energy I thought I would not need to breathe for days.

Annie Dillard

Service Wash

An old bag is folding clothes.

I can remember when pants were pants. You wore them for twenty years, then you cut them down for pan scrubs. Or quilts. We used to make lovely quilts out of Celanese bloomers. Every gusset a memory. Not bras. They won't lie flat. We didn't wear bras till after the war, round here. We stayed in and polished the lino.

I didn't see an Oxo cube till I was twenty-five. That's when I got my glasses. And we weren't having hysterectomies every two minutes either, like the girls these days. If something went wrong down below, you kept your gob shut and turned up the wireless.

We never got woken with a teasmade. We were knocked up every morning by a man with a six-foot pole. It wasn't all fun. We'd no showers. We used to club together and send the dirtiest one to the Slipper Baths. We might have been mucky but we had clean slippers.

And it was all clogs. Clogs on cobbles - you could hardly hear yourself coughing up blood. Clogs - when times were hard we had them for every meal, with condensed milk, if we were lucky.

And no one had cars. If you wanted to get run over, you'd to catch a bus to the main road. And of course, corner shop was the only one with gas, so you'd to go cap in hand if you wanted to gas yourself.

For years we had to make our own rugs. We used to stitch mice on to pieces of sacking. We weren't always making jokes either. I once passed a remark about parsnips and couldn't sit down for a week.

Oh, but I shall never forget the Coronation. 1953. We all crammed into the one front room and stared at this tiny grey picture. Somebody had cut it out of the paper - nobody got television till the year after.

I think we were more neighbourly. If anyone was ill in bed, the whole street would let themselves in and ransack the parlour.

And we didn't do all this keep-fit. We got our exercise lowering coffins out of upstairs windows. In fact, if people were very heavy we used to ask them to die downstairs.

It wasn't all gloom. My brother went to Spain, which was very unusual in those days. Mind you, that was the Civil War, and he got shot for trying to paddle.

We couldn't afford holidays. Sometimes us kids would take some dry bread and a bottle of water and sit in the TB clinic, but that was about it.

We had community spirit round here, right to the end. The day they demolished our street it was like the war all over again - dead bodies, hands sticking out of the rubble. The council should have let us know.

That's me done, best be off. Got a bit of cellular blanket for my supper, don't want it to spoil. Ta-ra ...

Victoria Wood

THIS IS HOW IT WAS

I Was Proceeding in a North-Easterly Direction -- ->

True Stories

After the trial of Fernando Garcia Marquez the Puerto Rican bandit, was interrupted when penal guard Luis Acevedo fired a shot into the ceiling of the courtroom "to keep the public in order", three people were taken to hospital suffering from shock.

But when the judge, Alvarado Ginorio, sentenced Mr Marquez to 495 years and 90 days, the courtroom, "which was full of the prisoner's relatives", broke into song and dance.

Fining 18-year-old Mr Davis Ticker of Exeter £100 for stealing £10 from the till at Millet's store in Exeter, the magistrate said: "I realise you had overspent on your credit cards by £1,000 and I have decided to deal leniently with you because you are now employed as a trainee financial consultant."

"There were some 50 of us singing away at the Harvest Festival service," said Mrs Lucy Ford of Havant. "Then this rather badly dressed man came into the church, walked up to the table on which the Harvest Offerings had been placed, and began to eat them.

"When he had finished the fruit and most of the vegetables, he produced an opener and opened a tin of Marrowbone Jelly. When Canon Brown asked him if he was enjoying himself, he said "I prefer Kit-e-Kat."

In a statement after the police had removed the man, Canon Brown said: "I have been a priest for 40 years and I have never seen anything like that before."

Christopher Logue

'I was on a bus to Washington, D.C. ...'

I was on a bus to Washington, D.C. Two days I'd been traveling and I was tired, tired, tired. The woman sitting next to me, a German with a ticket good for anywhere, never stopped yakking. I understood little of what she said but what I did understand led me to believe that she was utterly deranged.

She finally took a breather when we hit Richmond. It was late at night. The bus threaded its way through dismal streets toward the bus station. We rounded a corner and there beneath a street light stood a white man and black woman. The woman wore a yellow dress and held a baby. Her head was thrown back in laughter. The man was red-haired, rough looking, and naked to the waist. His skin seemed luminous. He was grinning at the woman, who watched him closely even as she laughed. Broken glass glittered at their feet.

There is something between them, something in the instant itself, that makes me sit up and stare. What is it, what's going on here? Why can't I ever forget them? Tell me, for God's sake, but make it snappy - I'm tired, and the bus is picking up speed, and the lunatic beside me is getting ready to say something.

Tobias Wolff

Solo Tackle

First version

I was a member of the Evander Tigers football team.
I still remember the first solo tackle I ever had.
It was against the Monroe team, Monroe were driving down the field. The men on our line were getting blown. Everytime their running back ran for a few yards he would start yelling.

There is one guy on the line from our team the Monroe guy kept yelling at him, telling him, "Next time I'm going to make you eat the ball." Frank the guy on our team just stood there and laughed.

Then it came my first solo tackle, the line got blown, the running back busts through the line and I see him coming. I'm the only guy that can stop him from scoring a touch down. He's about twenty yards from the goal line.

Finally he comes close enough for me to tackle, but all of a sudden he sticks his hand against my cage. Then I just grabbed his shoulder pads and throw him on the ground. I rolled and stood over him, from the sidelines I hear Coach Kalman yell "Look at Figueroa"!! And that's when I made my first solo tackle.

Second version

"Next time I am going to make you eat the ball," the Monroe players yelled. The Monroe players were mad. They were really losing bad. The score was 38 to 0 - and we were playing on their own field, so they had to score. Monroe was driving down the field. The men on our line were getting blown right out of their cleats.

Every time the running back ran for a few yards he would start yelling. Frank would just look at him and laugh. I finally got the chance to prove myself to the coach and the team. I knew if I made an interception or a tackle the team would finally accept me. So I had to go all out. I had to be all over the field, and I was. But someone would always cut in front of me and make the tackle. Finally the running back bust through the line and I saw him coming. There is one guy in front of him to block me, but he just runs by him. So it's only me and him, and I am the only one who can stop him from scoring. He is about twenty yards from the goal line. He comes close and I feel confident, cause I know I have to make the tackle.

He is in my range. All of a sudden he sticks his hand on my cage. As a counter action I grab his shoulder pads and jersey and throw him on the ground. I roll over on the ground and stand over him and look down at him. As I am standing over him I hear the coach yell, "Look at Figueroa"! After the tackle I felt proud. I felt twenty feet tall, and that I could tackle anybody that came in my way. And that was my first solo tackle.

Ramon Figueroa

Travelling in a Comfortable Car

Travelling in a comfortable car
Down a rainy road in the country
We saw a ragged fellow at nightfall
Signal to us for a ride, with a low bow.
We had a roof and we had room and we drove on
And we heard me say in a grumpy voice: no
We can't take anyone with us.
We had gone on a long way, perhaps a day's march
When suddenly I was shocked by this voice of mine
This behaviour of mine and this
Whole world.

Bertolt Brecht

The Fire of London

[September 2nd, 1666]
River full of lighters and boats taking in goods, and good goods swimming in the water, and only I observed that hardly one lighter or boat in three that had the goods of a house in, but there was a pair of Virginalls in it ... walked to my boat; and there upon the water again, and to the fire up and down, it still encreasing, and the wind great. So near the fire as we could for smoke; and all over the Thames, with one's face in the wind, you were almost burned with a shower of fire-drops. This is very true; so as houses were burned by these drops and flakes of fire, three or four, nay, five or six houses, one from another. When we could endure no more upon the water, we to a little ale-house on the Bankside, over against the Three Cranes, and there staid till it was dark almost, and saw the fire grow; and, as it grew darker, appeared more and more, and in corners and upon steeples, and between churches and houses, as far as we could see up the hill of the City, in a most horrid malicious bloody flame, not like the fine flame of an ordinary fire . . . We staid till, it being darkish, we saw the fire as only one entire arch of fire from this to the other side of the bridge, and in a bow up the hill for an arch above a mile long: it made me weep to see it. The churches, houses, and all on fire and flaming at once; and a horrid noise the flames made, and the cracking of houses at their ruine. So home with a sad heart, and there find every body discoursing and lamenting the fire.

A Prize-Fight

[May 7th, 1667]
So to my chamber, and there did some little business, and then abroad, and stopped at the Bear-garden-stairs, there to see a prize fought. But the house so full there was no getting in there, so forced to go through an alehouse into the pit, where the bears are baited; and upon a stool did see them fight; which they did very furiously, a butcher and a waterman. The former had the better all along, till by and by the latter dropped his sword out of his hand, and the butcher, whether not seeing his sword dropped I know not, but did give him a cut over the wrist, so as he was disabled to fight any longer. But, Lord! to see how in a minute the whole stage was full of watermen to revenge the foul play, and the butchers to defend their fellow, though most blamed him; and there they all fell to it knocking down and cutting many on each side. It was pleasant to see, but that I stood in the pit, and feared that in the tumult I might get some hurt. At last the rabble broke up, and so I away to White Hall and so to St. James's.

Samuel Pepys

Working from a Photograph

Pete Skingley

Comparative Methods of Medicine

Let God be praised: if a man understands the affairs of the Franks, he can only praise the Almighty for the diversity of his creatures, and sanctify His name; for he finds they are only beasts endowed with the virtues of courage and fighting spirit, and no others, just as beasts have the virtue of strength and the power to bear burdens. Let me then tell something of their affairs and the strangeness of their minds.

Here is a story of their strange practices in the art of medicine: the Lord of al-Munaytara once wrote to my uncle asking him to send him a physician to treat the sick among his people; so he sent him a Christian physician called Thabit. He came back to us after less than ten days and we exclaimed "You have been very quick!" He told us the following story. "They brought me two patients, a knight with an abscess in the leg, and a woman afflicted with hallucinations. I put a poultice on the knight's leg and the abscess burst and became well. As for the woman, I put her on a diet, and kept her humour moist (i.e. by putting cold presses on her head to counteract the overheated brain). Then a Frankish doctor arrived, and said "This man does not know how to treat these cases." Then he spoke to the knight, "Which would you prefer, to live a one-legged man, or to keep them both and die?" The knight replied that he would rather lose one leg and live. So the doctor told them to summon a strong knight with a sharp axe. Then - and this happened in my presence - he put the patient's leg on the stump of a tree, and said to the knight, "Now strike the leg with your axe and cut it off at one blow!" I saw him strike a blow which failed to sever the leg; then he struck a second blow at which the marrow spurted out of the bone and the patient died immediately.

The physician then looked at the woman and said "This woman has a devil in her head, who is in love with her; shave her hair off." This was done, and the woman began once more to eat articles of their diet such as garlic and mustard. Her disorder got worse, and the physician declared that the devil had got into her head. He took a razor and made an incision on her head in the shape of a cross, then he flayed the skin off the middle of the incision, so the bone of the skull was exposed, which he rubbed with salt. The woman immediately died. I asked "Have you any further need of me?" They answered "No"; so I came away, having learned things unknown to me before in the practice of medicine.

Ousama

Ingrafting the Small-pox

A propos of distempers, I am going to tell you a thing that I am sure will make you wish yourself here. The small-pox, so fatal, and so general amongst us, is here entirely harmless by the invention of *ingrafting* which is the term they give it. There is a set of old women who make it their business to perform the operation every autumn, in the month of September, when the great heat is abated. People send to one another to know if any of their family has a mind to have the small-pox; they make parties for this purpose, and when they are met (commonly fifteen or sixteen together), the old woman comes with a nutshell full of the matter of the best sort of small-pox and asks what veins you please to have opened. She immediately rips open that you offer to her with a large needle (which gives you no more pain than a common scratch), and puts into the vein as much venom as can lie on the head of her needle, and after binds up the little wound with a hollow bit of shell; and in this manner opens up four or five veins. The Grecians have commonly the superstition of opening one in the middle of the forehead, in each, and on the breast, to mark the sign of the cross; but this has a very ill effect, all these wounds leaving little scars, and is not done by those that are not superstitious, who choose to have them in the legs, or that part of the arm that is concealed. The children or young patients play together all the rest of the day, and are in perfect health to the eighth. Then the fever begins to seize them, and they keep their beds two days, very seldom three. They have very rarely above twenty or thirty in their faces, which never mark; and in eight days' time they are well as before their illness. Where they are wounded, there remain running sores during the distemper, which I don't doubt is a great relief to it. Every year thousands undergo this operation; and the French ambassador says pleasantly, that they take the small-pox here by way of diversion, as they take the waters in other countries. There is no example of any one that has died of it; and you may believe I am very well satisfied of the safety of this experiment, since I intend to try it on my dear little son.

I am a patriot enough to take pains to bring this useful invention into fashion in England; and I should not fail to write to some of our doctors very particularly about it, if I knew any one of them that I thought had virtue enough to destroy such a considerable branch of their revenue for the good of mankind. But that distemper is too beneficial to them not to expose to all their resentment the hardy wight that should undertake to put an end to it. Perhaps, if I live to return, I may, however, have courage to war with them.

Lady Mary Wortley Montagu

Description of Cells

I took a good clear piece of cork, and with a Pen-knife sharpened as keen as a Razor, I cut a piece of it off, and thereby left the surface of it exceeding smooth; then examining it very diligently with a Microscope, me thought I could perceive it to appear a little porous; but I could not so plainly distinguish them as to be sure that they were pores, much less what Figure they were of: But judging from the lightness and yielding quality of Cork, that certainly the texture could not be so curious but that possibly, if I could use some further diligence, I might find it to be discernable with a Microscope. I with the same sharp Pen-knife, cut off from the former smooth surface an exceeding thin piece of it, and placing it on a black object Plate, because it was itself a white body, and casting the light on it with a deep plano-convex glass I could exceedingly plainly perceive it to be all perforated and porous, much like a Honey-comb, but that the pores of it were not regular ....

But, to return to our Observation. I told several lines of these pores and found that there were usually about three-score of these small cells placed endways in the eighteenth part of an Inch in length, whence I concluded there must be near eleven hundred of them or somewhat more than a thousand in the length of an Inch, and therefore in a square inch above a Million, or 1,166,400, and in a Cubic Inch, above twelve hundred Million or 1,259,712,000 a thing almost incredible, did not our Microscope assure us of it by ocular demonstration; - So prodigiously curious are the works of Nature ...

Nor is this kind of Texture peculiar to Cork only; for upon examination with my Microscope, I have found that the pith of an Elder, or almost any other Tree, the inner pulp or pith of the Cany hollow stalks of several other Vegetables: as of Fennel, Carrots, Daucus, Bur-docks, Teasels, Fearn, and some kinds of Reeds, etc. have much such a kind of Schematism, as I have lately shewn that of Cork, save only that here the pores are rang'd the long-ways, or the same way with the length of the Cane, whereas in Cork they are Transverse.

But though I could not with my Microscope, nor with my breath, nor any other way I have yet try'd, discover a passage out of one of those cavities into another, yet cannot thence conclude, that therefore there are none such, by which the *succus nutritius*, or appropriate juices of vegetables, may pass through them; for in several of these vegetables, whil'st green, I have with my Microscope, plainly enough discover'd these Cells or Pores fill'd with juices, and by degrees sweating them out.

Now, though I have with great diligence endeavoured to find whether there be any such thing in those Microscopic pores of Wood or Piths as the Valves in the heart, veins, and other passages in animals, that open and give passage to the contain'd fluid juices one way, and shut themselves, and impede the passage of such liquors back again, yet I have not hitherto been able to say anything positive in it; though, me thinks, it seems very probable, that Nature has in these passages, as well as in those of Animal bodies, very many appropriated Instruments and contrivances, whereby to bring her designs and ends to pass, which 'tis not improbable but that some diligent Observer, if help'd with better Microscopes, may in time detect.

Robert Hooke

Photojournalism

Letter from a Diplomat to his Wife

H.N. to V.S-W.   17th June 1938
4 King's Bench Walk E.C.4

I met an Austrian yesterday who had just got away from Vienna, and what he said made me ill. There is a devilish sort of humour in their cruelty. For instance, they rounded up the people walking in the Prater on Sunday last, and separated the Jews from the rest. They made the Jewish gentlemen take off all their clothes and walk on all fours on the grass. They made the old Jewish ladies get up into the trees by ladders and sit there. They then told them to chirp like birds. The Russians never committed atrocities like that. You may take a man's life; but to destroy all his dignity is bestial. This man told me that with his own eyes he had seen Princess Stahrenberg washing out the urinals at the Vienna railway-station. The suicides have been appalling. A great cloud of misery hangs over the town.

   I might have thought the man exaggerating. His facts were detailed and his manner calm. But still I retained a portion of doubt whether even Germans could behave like this. But I dined with Bernstorff and when I repeated these stories, he said, "Yes, they are true. A Nazi friend of mine was attached to German Headquarters. He told me that he couldn't stand it. He said, 'I have seen grown men behave like little boys who pull the wings off flies.'"

   Dearest, what unhappiness there is in this world. I am glad I am in a position to do something, however slight, to help. I simply could not just remain idle and do nothing.

Harold Nicolson

Extract from a Journal Kept Whilst in Hospital

The women in here

CK - aged 59, lives in Mafeking Street, worked 'temporarily' at Rowntrees for 30 years, 15 hours a week, packing Black Magic.

   Her first husband died when he was 45 having said he would. She has a son and a daughter; the son went to the secondary modern, got 7 O-levels and became an export manager for Rowntrees against University graduates by saying I'm going to show these graduates they're not necessarily best.

   Told stories of her mother-in-law. This woman was left motherless at 11 with 4 younger brothers and sisters to bring up. She married at 16 and had four kids by the time she was 20. "I was that green I didn't know what caused it, I'd rather bake a stone of bread than sleep wi' 'im". Then she got the birth rate down a bit and had 3 more,

5 boys who lived and two girls both of whom went down with cot deaths at 14 months. Her first husband she found dead in bed when she tried to get his cold feet off her as she fed the baby.

CK remembers her father going out in the 30s to heckle blackshirts, her mother frightened. He said he was going to let them know what he thought. Her father fought in Egypt in the First World War, went into the reserves and was called up when she was 11 in 1939. She didn't see him again properly until the end of the war when she was 17. Her mother got a telegram to say he was missing, presumed dead, at Dunkirk. Her mother had Christine and the other kids sleeping in the same room as her, herself and the elder one in the double bed and the two young ones head to toe on a single mattress they'd dragged into the front bedroom.

In the middle of the night there was a loud knocking on the door. The mother got up, told the kids to get under the sideboard, took the big poker from the fire irons that they called Aunt Kate (after a very tall aunt) and went to the door expecting the Germans. "I'm taking one of 'em with me, any road!"

It was her husband. He had found his own way up from the South Coast.

Angela Fisher

The Indian Rebellion

Household Arrangements in Besieged Lucknow, 1857

Thursday, 20 August. A good deal of shelling has been going on this morning, but it is mostly our own ... It rained in the evening a good deal. A poor little child next door to us died of cholera; it was only taken ill about one o'clock and it was dead before seven. The poor mother was in a dreadful state just before it died, and afterwards perfectly calm. While we were undressing she came and asked if we had an empty box we could give her to bury the poor little thing in. We had not one long enough ...

Thursday, 27 August. Colonel Inglis had a most merciful escape last night. He was standing on the bastion at Mr Gubbins's house, close to Mr Webb when he was killed. They saw the round shot coming, and went down to avoid it, but it hit Mr Webb, and a native who was with him, killing them both instantaneously. It makes one shudder to think how death is hovering about and around us all; busy indeed has he been amongst this little garrison. Mrs Thornhill had a little girl last night. Sir Henry Lawrence's things are being sold today (he had recently been killed); heard of a ham being sold for £7 and a tin of soup sufficient only for one day's dinner for £1.5s.!!! Money has ceased to be of any value, and people are giving unheard-of prices for stores of any kind - one dozen brandy £20; one small box of vermicelli, £5; four small cakes of chocolate, £2.10s.!!! ...

Monday, 5 October. Today we have begun to restrict ourselves to two chuppatties each a day; and soon, I fear, we shall have to eat horseflesh; but as yet we have beef and rice. I have been hungry today, and could have eaten more, had I had it. Seven men and three officers came in today from the Fureed Bux, badly wounded. Mrs Roberts came to see us this morning, and told us the chloroform at the hospital is all gone. Mrs Omiley's children both died in one hour a day or two ago ...

Sunday, 18 October. We have been out of soap for some days and are now obliged to wash with what is called 'bason' (ground grain made into a paste with water). It is a nice clean thing, and the best substitute for soap.

Adelaide Case

One Less Octopus at Paxos

We were at our regular swimming-place which is partly pebbly beach and partly big flat rocks when there came along in the shallows among the rocks by the shore a stocky young woman in a hooded wet-suit top with a diving mask and a snorkel and flippers and a speargun and a big sheath-knife strapped to her right leg. She was nosing among the underwater rocks in an ardent and serious way like a dog at a rabbit hole. She fired the speargun, then held up the spear with an octopus writhing on it. It was a mottled pinky-brown and its head was about as big as two clasped hands.

    She slid it off the spear, grabbed it by a couple of tentacles, and beat it again and again on a flat rock, spattering briny drops each time. The octopus clung to the rock with its free tentacles; they came away with sounds like kisses as she peeled it off the rock and put it into a plastic bag.

    She had pushed up her mask and pushed back her hood. She had a dark face, a serious look and a heavy frown. She had short dark curling hair. She had a squeeze-bottle of detergent; a bystander explained that she'd squirted it into the octopus's hiding-place in the rocks to make it come out (not being able to breathe) and be speared by her.

    Later I found myself imagining that young woman's preparations for her trip to Paxos. l saw her at the windows of travel agents, I saw her turning the pages of brochures, I saw her looking at octopus pictures in books. I saw her marking off days on a calendar. I saw her at the supermarket, picking up bottles of detergent and reading their labels. I saw her packing her wet-suit, her mask and snorkel, her flippers, her speargun, her knife, her bottle of detergent. I saw her in the underground, sitting up straight with a serious face, going to

Victoria. Her luggage was a rucksack and a diver's bag made of heavy PVC. I saw her on the train to Gatwick. I saw her checking in at the airline counter. I saw her on the plane to Corfu eating breakfast with a serious face, perhaps reading a diving magazine.

I saw her on the boat from Corfu to Paxos looking steadfastly at the sun-points on the water and watching for the shape of the island.

I saw her in her room unpacking the wet-suit, the mask and snorkel, the flippers, the speargun, the knife, the bottle of detergent. I saw her sitting on the bed looking down at her naked feet.

Russell Hoban

South African Journal

Our last day in South Africa

Our last day in South Africa. We chatted to Miriam the maid before leaving. She'd been here since 7am cleaning the oven, washing up the breakfast things, sweeping the floor. We'd told her our names but she insisted on calling us 'master' and 'madam'. I didn't like it - made me feel like the Queen! I asked where she lived and what other families she worked for. She said she really wanted to give up work as she was getting old, but she had five grandchildren to support who lived in the Transkei - her two daughters had been murdered in the 'troubles'. She looked weary and resigned. I wanted to hug her, but I didn't know how she'd respond, so instead I shook her hand and said I hoped things worked out well for her.

I sat in the car and sniffed for the next couple of hours. I told the others I was getting a cold. Everyone very quiet.

We've seen so much of this. I remembered Seraphina the Hayward's maid, who got up at 5.30 am every morning, prepared the breakfast for her own three kids and got them ready for school and set out from the township at 6.30 to travel to the Haywards' house which took her an hour by black taxi. And how when there was a strike called by the radical young blacks - who were armed, and they blockaded the roads in and out of the township, Seraphina got up in the dark and slipped out and walked 7 miles across country so that she could help her 'mistress' (who'd had a stroke) get dressed and prepare her breakfast. What makes these women so reliable and devoted that they risk death to go to work? For 140 Rand (£30) a month! I thought of the 10 Rand (£2) we'd left her as a tip for doing our washing and the Haywards said she was delighted and did a little dance round the kitchen. I could just imagine her doing that - she had a wonderfully broad bottom.

And then there'd been all the stories of our friend Maggie's coloured maid Carrie, who was, 'so tiny but very bright and could turn her hand to anything. She'd have really gone places if she'd had the opportunities'. Carrie had been taught to read by Maggie's 7 year old son, but her own 7 year old child, being brought up by her sister back home, died of meningitis because no one realised what was wrong with her. Carrie only got to see her once a month. What kind of society is it that doesn't allow women to bring up their own children?

And Gladys, the Rawdon's maid, with her beautiful baby Sam that she was feeding on the carpet the night we came home from the restaurant. Gladys had a broad open face and smiled a lot. She laughed when she told us about Sam's birth. (He was her 7th, most, apparently, by different fathers.) The Rawdons had kept saying to her "Gladys, you're getting very fat, you must lose weight" but she never let on she was pregnant because she didn't want to lose her job. At 7 months she went to the clinic and they said her blood pressure was so high she had to go in for an emergency Caesarian straight away. She said she was lucky because the Rawdons hadn't dismissed her. Sam slept during the day in her room by the garage so that she could get on with her work and woke at night. She did complain of always being very tired. What irony when the Rawdons, with their Hollywood style house and swimming pool and three cars and one school age child and a wife who doesn't work - and yet Gladys doesn't want to lose her job and there is no one else to support her family. Her other six children are being brought up by her elderly father, and mother who's a bit dotty. It takes her 9 hours to get home once a month by bus, and then a walk of two hours into the hills in Zululand. She doesn't want to give up Sam to her parents but how can she work once he starts to walk? Traditionally in African societies the family was strong. Apartheid and the Group Areas Act have between them ripped it apart.

Eve Rawdon told us that she had tried to get Gladys to go to a Family Planning Clinic. Apparently Gladys, on a friend's advice, had been taking Epsom salts to prevent pregnancy. All the whites go on about the blacks not using birth control and how they can't support the children they have. (Black South Africans have one of the fastest growing birthrates in Africa, whilst the white population is static.) But if you've got nothing, what is there to lose? Relationships become your only source of wealth. People aren't rational about having babies anywhere. Look at my own parents. They had me straight after the war when they had nowhere to live. The rooms they eventually found they had to leave when my brother was born because the owners didn't want two children living there.

Sitting in the plush Carlton Hotel in Johannesburg before getting a flight, I find myself being excessively polite to the black waiters. Tainted with white guilt. I shall be glad to go home. This country's a mess, a beautiful, terrible mess.

I can't stand it any more - ironies, contradictions, dilemmas and terrible divisions between black and white. And yet there is the image of those black women - their strength and dignity and laughter. As all our white liberal friends said "You do the best you can". Those African maids were doing their best. Quietly and without making any fuss, they got on with bringing up other people's children and cleaning other people's houses. But how do you begin to change all that and how do you heal the pain? A friend had said on our last evening "What we all fear is that in the 'New South Africa' someone will point the finger at us and say 'But you could have done more'". Yes - that's true for us all. I left the waiters a large tip.

Barbara Webb

SHORT STORIES

1997: The Illegal Immigrant

For an eternity, the man floundered, tossed about in the freezing chill of the waves. All around him was a black night, and the black sea. His limbs, numb with cold and pain, flailed helplessly against the heaving waves. Barely conscious, he clung to the plank of wood with a maniacal strength. Once again, a tower of water crashed down upon him and the sharp needles of cold rain drove into his skull. He felt his leg hit something - a rock. Helpless and despairing, he cried out.

When he awoke, he found himself lying on the ground, salt water and blood caked on his lips and the tide pulling restlessly at his ankles. A tuft of hard grass pressed irritatingly into his side and the splinters of his plank lay about him. It was still night and the outline of the hills above him were strange and unfamiliar but far, far away, in the distance, he could make out lights the colours of the rainbow. They were blue and red but mostly yellow; pillars of yellow shimmering lights, like the palaces of the gods, where the people of the free country live. For a moment, hope filled him. Enraptured, he gazed towards the hazy glittering horizon, oblivious to the piercing cold and the wounds of his body.

Suddenly, out of the silence, came the sound of dogs barking and shouts, faint but ominous. He had heard of soldiers here who would drag him back to the place he had left. He looked up, eyes wide with terror, to the top of the hill. High up on the hillside, he saw beams of different lights, cruel white lights everywhere that tore crazily over the surface of the slope, slicing the cold air and looking for him, he knew.

He scrambled up, shivering, the harsh reality returning to him, and thrashed wildly through the undergrowth away from the lights. Half running, half crawling, he was a hunted animal, stumbling on uneven ground and loose pebbles, splashing through mud. His breath whistled painfully through his nostrils and he sobbed hysterically. It was the same hell he had felt in the water, endless, dark and panic-stricken.

Suddenly, the trees broke apart and he hurtled onto ground that was hard and rough. A road. In front loomed the black silent silhouette of a van and human figures moved round quickly and hissed urgently, in his own dialect, "Come. Come to us. We have been waiting for you." For a moment, he thought of soldiers and demons but then he realized that these were the people who would take him to the free country. He had paid his money. He lurched towards them, the mouth of the vehicle opened and rough hands pushed him through. The doors were slammed behind and the van started to rock crazily. He lay prostrate on the floor, caring nothing for the shakes and jerks as they drove forward, rolling about the feet of those who had come.

He was conscious suddenly of a warm heat on his neck and opened his eyes. For a moment, his heart leapt because he did not know where he was. Looking around, he saw a tiny room; the bunk on which he lay took up more than half its space and was underneath a window. The floor was covered with coils of thick rope, rusty oil cans and miscellaneous bundles and he lay on a hard wooden board with no covering or sheet except the warm sun streaming through the dust. The door was closed. Then he knew. He was in the palaces of the gods.

Crawling stiffly to the window, he peered out. His mind reeled at the height of his room and terrified, he almost drew back. Then he saw his first look of the country which he had hoped so much from, where all were rich and free. The street below was filthy, grey with refuse, trodden and soggy. The air was thick and heavy with heat and humidity, dust and fumes and the light was blinding. Vehicles crammed the street, honking and tooting. A crushed chicken lay by the side of the road, its head a formless mass, its feathers dull and bedraggled in the sewer. Somewhere below a baby shrieked, a wireless blared and the shouts of a fight flared up.

Bewildered, the man looked closer at the scene before him and saw a shrivelled Chinese woman, rummaging in a large yellow tin barrel. Her face was lined with dirt and age, her clothes ragged and her long grey hair lay heavily down her back, a solid mass congealed with sweat and filth. Her eyes were filled with a dreadful passivity as she sought for discarded waste with her dry, black rimmed fingers, in the rubbish bin.

This was the country of the Free.

Isobel Jacobs

Nicole and the Giant Cake

I was in bed when my Mother shouted up the stairs "There's a letter for you Nicole with 'IMPORTANT' stamped all over it." "Alright I'm coming its probably another order" I said (my Mother is called Kathy I am sixteen years old I'm a baker it is the year 1971). I came sliding down the bannister and jumped onto the hall floor. Kathy gave me the letter I opened it and inside this is what it said.

Buckingham Palace

Dear Nicole,

I am having a party at the palace and I am going to have a big feast but unfortunately my Chief Cook has resigned so will you please come and fill in the space. I need a big giant cake baking, a cake big enough to feed nine hundred and seventy eight hungry people. I have four maids, four cooks, two waiters and two butlers, all waiting to be told what to do. Will you please write an answer back, if you want to come, come on the first of January at four o'clock in the afternoon.

Yours sincerely
The Queen

"Mother its a letter from the Queen asking me whether I want to be Chief Cook at the palace, can I?" I said. "Of course you can if you want to" said Mother "Write an answer straight away" so I went upstairs and wrote an answer. This is what I put.

58 Shay Drive
London

Dear Queen

I would be delighted to come to the palace and be Chief Cook.
I will be there at four o'clock on January the first.

Yours sincerely
Nicole

I was really pleased that I had been asked but there was one snag if the cake was going to be a big cake it would need a big oven, and big mixers everything would have to be bought, unless the Queen had some very big mixers and ovens. So I told my Dad and he said "I don't know of any big giant mixers and ovens but I will look around." Then there was a knock at the door "rater-tat-tat". I opened it, it was Joanne Randel asking me if I was playing. I said "Yes, why don't we go and play in the woods". So we did. When we got there I told Joanne about my offer from the Queen. Joanne said "Why don't you make your own oven and mixer". "What a good idea, we will try that" I said. Then Joanne went home for her dinner.

The next day I packed my clothes it was December the thirty first my last day at home.

On January the first I caught a red bus at seven o'clock a.m. it smelt of cigarettes, but it wasn't so bad. When I got to the palace I had to persuade the guards to let me through the gate. I was just wondering where to go, when the Queen came along a corridor and said "I will show you around the palace, follow me." Then with a swish of her robes she walked briskly towards the kitchen. We went through lots and lots of passages and corridors covered with tapestries and paintings till at last we came to the kitchen. The Queen showed me around and said "Stand in your order please", then she turned to me and said "The first four girls are the maids, the next are the cooks, then the waiters and last but not least the two butlers." "Now then I will say their names in the order that they are standing in, Kate, Joey, Julie, Rachel, Nicola, Ruth, Julia, Vicky, Timothy, John, Robert, Peter." "Everyone this is Nicole, she is your new Chief Cook". Then the Queen left me to myself. I said "Well then let's start finding the ingredients for the giant cake." So I, Rachel and Ruth put the ingredients in a big bowl while Kate, Joey and Julie got the ingredients for us. We put in the big bowl

    ten bags of flour
    seven eggs
    six packets of raisins
    one tin of cocoa powder
    three packets of butter
    four pounds of salt
    and ten drops of peppermint

When I and Rachel and Ruth had put all that in we looked around for a big mixer but there wasn't one. So I sent Peter up to ask the Queen if there were any big mixers in the palace. He came down with the answer. "The Queen will be coming down shortly" that was a relief the Queen would be able to do something about it. The Queen came down a minute later I said "Have you got any big giant mixers for us to use dear Queen?" "Yes, as a matter of fact we have I ordered them a week ago for the giant cake. Timothy, John, Peter and Robert will you come and get them, follow me." We waited and waited till Timothy, John, Peter and Robert came panting through

PROBLEMS INVOLVED IN MAKING A GIANT CAKE...

the kitchen door carrying two giant mixers and one giant oven. We put the mixers in a corner of the room and then we got back to work. The mixture was put in the mixer and then Nicola switched it on, there was a big whirring sound as the mixer turned round and round faster and faster then suddenly "Crash!!" one mixer broke into little bits and the cake mixture flew everywhere. Kate, Joey, Julie and Rachel all said "Oh" Nicola, Ruth, Julia and Vicky all said "Eee" and Timothy, Robert, Peter, John and I just stood there in amazement. We slowly stooped down and picked up all the mixture which had flowed out of the mixer (when it broke) and put it in the other one. Then I said "Julie and Ruth will you please remove all of what's left of the mixer." When everything was back to normal, we started all over again. Whirr went the mixer round and round it went. Then Kate said "When do we stop it?" in a very loud voice. "About now" I answered back. So we stopped the mixer and then put the mixture for the giant cake in a giant cake tin. Then Robert and John put the cake in the giant oven. Julie turned the oven to number five on the oven and the giant cake started to cook. When the giant cake was cooked Joey and Vicky made the white icing and they put it on. Joey and Vicky had to stand on a very high chair to reach the top of the cake. I said "Kate and Rachel will you please go and tell the Queen that the giant cake is iced and made". So we waited and waited till Kate and Rachel came through the kitchen door with the Queen. The Queen said "We will have to get the cake through the door somehow", "But how are we going to do it" said Julia. "By pushing, heaving, pulling and trying hard" said the Queen. So we got the giant cake on its side and Kate, Joey, Julie, the Queen, Vicky, Rachel and I went round the other side of the door and Julia, Ruth, Nicola, Peter, John, Timothy and Robert pushed and pushed then suddenly! the cake went right through the door. "We're through, we're through" shouted Julie. That afternoon everything was set out on a table. (It was the party that the giant cake was for). When the guests had all sat down the Lord Mayoress said "Ladies, Gentlemen, Boys and Girls I am now going to cut this giant cake. Oh dear I can't reach the top of the cake will somebody please fetch me a high chair to stand on). I will now proudly cut this magnificent giant cake." Then when the Lord Mayoress stood on tiptoes to cut the cake SPLAT! she fell into the giant cake icing. Everyone gave a cry of horror the Queen said "Come with me Lady Mayoress, we will see what we can do for you". Then the Lord Mayor cut the cake safely and everyone had a piece (a big one too).

Then the children played games and the adults danced. After all the guests had gone the Queen came to me and said "Thank you so much, please will you make another giant cake the people liked it so much."

So it started all over again.

This is my own work and it is not a copy or near copy of anything I have read or heard.

Celia Milford

The Follower

Mrs Meade had been in the nursing home with heart trouble for three weeks, and her doctor, to whom she had confided the terror that obsessed her, had at last persuaded her to see the famous psycho-analyst, Dr Stone. She awaited his visit in great trepidation. It would not be easy to tell him of her fantastic experiences - hallucinations her own doctor insisted on calling them.

A quarter of an hour before the time when she expected Dr Stone, there was a knock on the door.

"I'm a little early, Mrs Meade," said a smooth voice from behind the screen, "and I must ask you to forgive my fancy dress ball appearance. I was very careless with a spirit lamp and am obliged to wear this mask for some time."

As he approached her bedside, Mrs Meade saw that her visitor's face was entirely concealed by a black mask with two small holes and a slit for his eyes and mouth.

"Now, Mrs Meade," he said, seating himself in a chair close to the bed. "I want you to tell me all about this mysterious trouble that is thought to be affecting your physical health. Please be perfectly frank with me. When did this - shall I say obsession - begin, and what precisely is it?"

"Very well," said Mrs Meade. "I will try to tell you the whole story. It began years ago - when I first went to live in Regent's Park. One afternoon I was most disagreeably struck by the appearance of a man who was loafing about outside the Baker Street Tube Station. I can't tell you how strong and horrible an impression he made on me. I can only say that there was something utterly hateful about his face, with its bold, malignant eyes - lashless eyes that searched me like unshaded lights. He seemed to leer at me with a "so there you are!" sort of look, and the queer thing was that, though I had never to my knowledge seen him and - as I say - his appearance came to me as a shock, yet it was not a shock of complete surprise. In the violent distaste I felt for him there was a faint element of - shall I say sub-concious recognition? - as though he reminded me of something I had once dreamt or imagined. I don't know! I vaguely noticed that he had on a black slouch hat and no tie but a sort of greenish muffler round his neck. Otherwise his clothes were ordinary. Like the description of Mr Hyde, he gave an impression of deformity without any nameable malformation. His face was horrible - moistly pale like ... like a toadstool! It's no good! I *can't* describe him! I can only repeat that the aversion he inspired in me was extraordinarily violent. I was conscious of his stare as I hurried past him and went down the steps, and it was a great relief to disappear into the lift and be whirled away in the Tube. Though I had plenty to do that day I could not quite dismiss him from my mind, and when I returned by

Tube late in the evening it was a horrid shock to find him lurking at the top of the steps just as though he were waiting for me. This time there was no doubt that he definitely leered at me, and I thought he faintly shook his head. I hurried past him. Soon I had that horrid sense of being followed and glanced over my shoulder. Sure enough, there he was - just a few paces behind! and, as I turned, he slightly raised his hat. I almost ran home, and I cannot say what a relief it was to hear my front door slam behind me. Well, I saw him the next day and the next, and practically every day. The distaste with which I recognized him became a definite shudder, and each time his cynical glance seemed to grow bolder. Several times he followed me towards my house, but never right up to the door. I made tentative inquiries at the little shops round the Tube Station, but no one seemed to have noticed him. The dread of meeting him became an absolute obsession. Soon I gave up going in the Tube and would make long detours in order to avoid that upper part of Baker Street."

"You minded him as much as all that, did you?" asked the doctor.

"Yes."

"Go on, don't let me interrupt you."

"For some time," continued Mrs Meade, "I did not see him and then there was a hideous incident. Returning from a walk in the park one day I saw quite a large crowd just outside the gate. A little girl had been run over. An ambulance man was carrying her lifeless form, and a policeman and some women were attending to the demented mother. Amongst all those shocked and pitying faces, suddenly I saw one vile, mocking face, its familiar features horribly distorted in a gloating grin. With positive glee he pointed at the dead child and then he turned *and leered at me*.

"After this horrible encounter you may be sure I shunned Upper Baker Street, but one day, just as I was starting to walk through the park, the heaviest rain I have ever seen came on, so I rushed towards the taxis at the top of the street and jumped into the first on the rank. A small boy opened the door for me, and, to avoid getting my hat wet, I gave him the address to give the driver. To my surprise we started off at a terrific pace. I looked up and saw a rather crouched back and a greenish muffler. The speed at which we were going was insane, and I banged on the window. The driver turned. Imagine my nightmare horror when I recognized that dreaded face, grinning at me through the glass. Heaven knows why we did not crash at once. Instead of watching the road, the creature on the box kept turning round to grin and gloat at me. We went faster and faster - whirling through the traffic. I was so sick with horror that, in spite of the appalling speed, I would at all costs have jumped out, but - struggle as I might - I could not turn the handle. I think I screamed and screamed and screamed. I was simply flung about the taxi. At last there was an appalling shock ....

"I can remember the tinkle of breaking glass and the awful pain in my head - and then no more.

"When I came to, I was in a hospital where for hours I had been unconscious from concussion. I began to ask questions but could only learn that I had been picked up from the debris of a taxi which had crashed into some railings, and that it was a miracle I had not been killed. As for the driver, he had unaccountably disappeared before the police arrived and no one claimed to have seen him. The taxi bore no number and could not be identified. The police were completely baffled.

"After this I insisted on leaving the neighbourhood, and made my husband take a house in Chelsea.

"Nearly a year passed and I began to hope that I should never see him again; but I became ill, and after endless consultations a very serious operation was decided on. Everything was arranged and the evening before the date fixed I drove to the nursing home with the sinking sensation natural to the occasion. I rang the bell and the door was promptly opened by a short man. I almost screamed. In spite of the incongruous livery, *it was him*! There he stood - sickly pale as ever, and with that awful, evil, *intimate* smile.

"In a wild panic, I sprang from the door and back into the taxi which was waiting with my luggage. Directly I got home I cancelled the operation. In spite of all the Harley Street opinions, I recovered. The operation was proved unnecessary."

Mrs Meade paused in her narrative. The listener spoke.

"Then this being - whatever he is - on this occasion may be said to have done you a good turn?" he asked.

"Yes," answered Mrs Meade," perhaps, but it didn't make me dread him any the less. Oh, the ghastly dreams I had! - that I had been given the anaesthetic and was thought to be unconscious, but I *wasn't*, and I saw the surgeon approach and, as he bent over me, his face was THE FACE!"

"Did you ever see him again, Mrs Meade?"

"I'm sorry," answered the patient hastily, "but the next time I saw him, I cannot tell you about. It is still too unbearable. There are things one cannot speak about. It was then I understood why he had pointed at that dead child and leered at me out of his vile little eyes. That was a long time ago, but the dread is always with me. You see, I still have one child left - I am always looking for what I fear. I can never leave my house without expecting to see him. What if one day I should meet him *in my house*?"

"I do not think you will ever do that, Mrs Meade."

"I suppose you think the whole thing is an illusion, Dr Stone? And in any case I don't suppose I have been able to give any impression of what - it - he - the creature is like," sighed Mrs Meade.

The listener rose from his chair and leant over the invalid.

"Is - his - face - like this?" he asked, and, as he spoke, he whipped off his mask.

No one who heard it will ever forget Mrs Meade's scream.

Two nurses rushed into her room, followed by Dr Stone, who, punctual to his appointment, had that moment arrived.

The dead woman lay on the bed.

There was no one else in the room.

Cynthia Asquith

Thank You, M'am

She was a large woman with a large purse that had everything in it but a hammer and nails. It had a long strap, and she carried it slung across her shoulder. It was about eleven o'clock at night, dark, and she was walking alone, when a boy ran up behind her and tried to snatch her purse. The strap broke with the sudden single tug the boy gave it from behind. But the boy's weight and the weight of the purse combined caused him to lose his balance. Instead of taking off full blast as he had hoped, the boy fell on his back on the sidewalk and his legs flew up. The large woman simply turned around and kicked him right square in his bluejeaned sitter. Then she reached down, picked the boy up by his shirt front, and shook him until his teeth rattled.

After that the woman said, "Pick up my pocketbook, boy, and give it here."

She still held him tightly. But she bent down enough to permit him to stoop and pick up her purse. Then she said, "Now ain't you ashamed of yourself?"

Firmly gripped by his shirt front, the boy said, "Yes'm."

The woman said, "What did you want to do it for?"

The boy said, "I didn't aim to."

She said, "You a lie!"

By that time two or three people passed, stopped, turned to look, and some stood watching.

"If I turn you loose, will you run?" asked the woman.

"Yes'm," said the boy.

"Then I won't turn you loose," said the woman. She did not release him.

"Lady, I'm sorry," whispered the boy.

"Um-hum! Your face is dirty. I got a great mind to wash your face for you. Ain't you got nobody home to tell you to wash your face?"

"No'm," said the boy.

"Then it will get washed this evening," said the large woman, starting up the street, dragging the frightened boy behind her.

He looked as if he were fourteen or fifteen, frail and willow-wild, in tennis shoes and blue jeans.

The woman said, "You ought to be my son. I would teach you right from wrong. Least I can do right now is to wash your face. Are you hungry?"

"No'm," said the being-dragged boy. "I just want you to turn me loose."

"Was I bothering *you* when I turned that corner?" asked the woman.

"No'm."

"But you put yourself in contact with *me*," said the woman. "If you think that that contact is not going to last awhile, you got another thought coming. When I get through with you, sir, you are going to remember Mrs Luella Bates Washington Jones."

Sweat popped out on the boy's face and he began to struggle. Mrs Jones stopped, jerked him around in front of her, put a half nelson about his neck, and continued to drag him up the street. When she got to her door, she dragged the boy inside, down a hall, and into a large kitchenette-furnished room at the rear of the house.

She switched on the light and left the door open. The boy could hear other roomers laughing and talking in the large house. Some of their doors were open, too, so he knew he and the woman were not alone. The woman still had him by the neck in the middle of her room.

She said, "What is your name?"

"Roger," answered the boy.

"Then, Roger, you go to that sink and wash your face," said the woman, whereupon she turned him loose - at last. Roger looked at the door - looked at the woman - looked at the door - *and went to the sink*.

"Let the water run until it gets warm," she said. "Here's a clean towel."

"You gonna take me to jail?" asked the boy, bending over the sink.

"Not with that face, I would not take you nowhere," said the woman. "Here I am trying to get home to cook me a bite to eat, and you snatch my pocketbook! Maybe you ain't been to your supper either, late as it be. Have you?"

"There's nobody home at my house," said the boy.

"Then we'll eat," said the woman. "I believe you're hungry - or been hungry - to try to snatch my pocketbook!"

"I want a pair of blue suede shoes," said the boy.

"Well, you didn't have to snatch *my* pocketbook to get some suede shoes," said Mrs Luella Bates Washington Jones. "You could of asked me."

"M'am?"

The water dripping from his face, the boy looked at her. There was a long pause. A very long pause. After he had dried his face, and not knowing what else to do, dried it again, the boy turned around, wondering what next. The door was open. He could make a dash for it down the hall. He could run, run, run, *run!*

The woman was sitting on the daybed. After a while she said, "I were young once and I wanted things I could not get."

There was another long pause. The boy's mouth opened. Then he frowned, not knowing he frowned.

The woman said, "Um-hum! You thought I was going to say *but*, didn't you? You thought I was going to say, *but I didn't snatch people's pocketbooks*. Well, I wasn't going to say that." Pause. Silence.

"I have done things, too, which I would not tell you, son - neither tell God if He didn't already know. Everybody's got something in common. So you set down while I fix us something to eat. You might run that comb through your hair so you will look presentable."

In another corner of the room behind a screen was a gas plate and an icebox. Mrs Jones got up and went behind the screen. The woman did not watch the boy to see if he was going to run now, nor did she watch her purse, which she left behind her on the daybed. But the boy took care to sit on the far side of the room, away from the purse, where he thought she could easy see him out the corner of her eye if she wanted to. He did not trust the woman *not* to trust him. And he did not want to be mistrusted now.

"Do you need somebody to go to the store," asked the boy, "maybe to get some milk or something?"

"Don't believe I do," said the woman, unless you just want sweet milk yourself. I was going to make cocoa out of this canned milk I got here."

"That will be fine," said the boy.

She heated some lima beans and ham she had in the icebox, made the cocoa, and set the table. The woman did not ask the boy anything about where he lived, or his folks, or anything else that would embarrass him. Instead, as they ate, she told him about her job in a hotel beauty shop that stayed open late, what the work was like, and how all kinds of women came in and out, blonds, redheads, and Spanish. Then she cut him a half of her ten-cent cake.

"Eat some more, son," she said.

When they were finished eating, she got up and said, "Now here, take this ten dollars and buy yourself some blue suede shoes. And next time, do not make the mistake of latching onto *my* pocketbook *nor nobody else's* - because shoes got by devilish ways will burn your feet. I got to get my rest now. But from here on in, son, I hope you will behave yourself."

She led him down the hall to the front door and opened it. "Good night! Behave yourself, boy!" she said, looking out into the street as he went down the steps.

The boy wanted to say something other than, "Thank you, M'am," to Mrs Luella Bates Washington Jones, but although his lips moved, he couldn't even say that as he turned at the foot of the barren stoop and looked up at the large woman in the door. Then she shut the door.

Langston Hughes

The Story of an Hour

Knowing that Mrs Mallard was afflicted with a heart trouble, great care was taken to break to her as gently as possible the news of her husband's death.

It was her sister Josephine who told her, in broken sentences; veiled hints that revealed in half concealing. Her husband's friend Richards was there, too, near her. It was he who had been in the newspaper office when intelligence of the railroad disaster was received, with Brently Mallard's name leading the list of "killed". He had only taken the time to assure himself of its truth by a second telegram, and had hastened to forestall any less careful, less tender friend in bearing the sad message.

She did not hear the story as many women have heard the same, with a paralyzed inability to accept its significance. She wept at once, with sudden, wild abandonment, in her sister's arms. When the storm of grief had spent itself she went away to her room alone. She would have no one follow her.

There stood, facing the open window, a comfortable, roomy armchair. Into this she sank, pressed down by a physical exhaustion that haunted her body and seemed to reach into her soul.

She could see in the open square before her house the top of trees that were all aquiver with the new spring life. The delicious breath of rain was in the air. In the street below a peddler was crying his wares. The notes of a distant song which some one was singing reached her faintly, and countless sparrows were twittering in the eaves.

There were patches of blue sky showing here and there through the clouds that had met and piled one above the other in the west facing her window.

She sat with her head thrown back across the cushion of the chair, quite motionless, except when a sob came up into her throat and shook her, as a child who has cried itself to sleep continues to sob in its dreams.

She was young, with a fair, calm face, whose lines bespoke repression and even a certain strength. But now there was a dull stare in her eyes, whose gaze was fixed away off yonder on one of those patches of blue sky. It was not a glance of reflection, but rather indicated a suspension of intelligent thought.

There was something coming to her and she was waiting for it, fearfully. What was it? She did not know; it was too subtle and elusive to name. But she felt it, creeping out of the sky, reaching toward her through the sounds, the scents, the color that filled the air.

Now her bosom rose and fell tumultuously. She was beginning to recognize this thing that was approaching to possess her, and she was striving to beat it back with her will - powerless as her two white tender hands would have been.

When she abandoned herself a little whispered word escaped her slightly parted lips. She said it over and over under her breath: "free, free, free!" The vacant stare and the look of terror that had followed it went from her eyes. They stayed keen and bright. Her pulses beat fast, and the coursing blood warmed and relaxed every inch of her body.

She did not stop to ask if it were or were not a monstrous joy that held her. A clear and exalted perception enabled her to dismiss the suggestion as trivial.

She knew that she would weep again when she saw the kind, tender hands folded in death; the face that had never looked save with love upon her, fixed and gray and dead. But she saw beyond that bitter moment a long procession of years to come that would belong to her absolutely. And she opened and spread her arms out to them in welcome.

There would be no one to live for her during those coming years; she would live for herself. There would be no powerful will bending hers in that blind persistence with which men and women believe they have a right to impose a private will upon a fellow-creature. A kind intention or a cruel intention made the act seem no less a crime as she looked upon it in that brief moment of illumination.

And yet she had loved him - sometimes. Often she had not. What did it matter! What could love, the unsolved mystery, count for in face of this possession of self-assertion which she suddenly recognized as the strongest impulse of her being!

"Free! Body and soul free!" she kept whispering.

Josephine was kneeling before the closed door with her lips to the key-hole, imploring for admission. "Louise, open the door! I beg; open the door - you will make yourself ill. What are you doing, Louise? For heaven's sake open the door."

"Go away. I am not making myself ill." No; she was drinking in a very elixir of life through that open window.

Her fancy was running riot along those days ahead of her. Spring days, and summer days, and all sorts of days that would be her own. She breathed a quick prayer that life might be long. It was only yesterday she had thought with a shudder that life might be long.

She arose at length and opened the door to her sister's importunities. There was a feverish triumph in her eyes, and she carried herself unwittingly like a goddess of Victory. She clasped her sister's waist, and together they descended the stairs. Richards stood waiting for them at the bottom.

Some one was opening the front door with a latchkey. It was Brently Mallard who entered, a little travel-stained, composedly carrying his grip-sack and umbrella. He had been far from the scene of the accident, and did not even know there had been one. He stood amazed at Josephine's piercing cry; at Richards' quick motion to screen him from the view of his wife.

But Richards was too late.

When the doctors came they said she had died of heart disease - of joy that kills.

Kate Chopin

The Blue Bouquet

I woke covered with sweat. Hot steam rose from the newly sprayed, red-brick pavement. A gray-winged butterfly, dazzled, circled the yellow light. I jumped from my hammock and crossed the room barefoot, careful not to step on some scorpion leaving his hideout for a bit of fresh air. I went to the little window and inhaled the country air. One could hear the breathing of the night, feminine, enormous. I returned to the center of the room, emptied water from a jar into a pewter basin, and wet my towel. I rubbed my chest and legs with the soaked cloth, dried myself a little, and, making sure that no bugs were hidden in the folds of my clothes, got dressed. I ran down the green stairway. At the door of the boardinghouse I bumped into the owner, a one-eyed taciturn fellow. Sitting on a wicker stool, he smoked, his eye half closed. In a hoarse voice, he asked:

"Where are you going?"

"To take a walk. It's too hot."

"Hmmm - everything's closed. And no streetlights around here. You'd better stay put."

I shrugged my shoulders, muttered "back soon," and plunged into the darkness. At first I couldn't see anything. I fumbled along the cobblestone street. I lit a cigarette. Suddenly the moon appeared from behind a black cloud, lighting a white wall that was crumbled in places. I stopped, blinded by such whiteness. Wind whistled slightly. I breathed the air of the tamarinds. The night hummed, full of leaves and insects. Crickets bivouacked in the tall grass. I raised my head: up there the stars too had set up camp. I thought that the universe was a vast system of signs, a conversation between giant beings. My actions, the cricket's saw, the star's blink, were nothing but pauses and syllables, scattered phrases from that dialogue. What word could it be, of which I was only a syllable? Who speaks the word? To whom is it spoken? I threw my cigarette down on the sidewalk. Falling, it drew a shining curve, shooting out brief sparks like a tiny comet.

I walked a long time, slowly. I felt free, secure between the lips that were at that moment speaking me with such happiness. The night was a garden of eyes. As I crossed the street, I heard someone come out of a doorway. I turned around, but could not distinguish anything. I hurried on. A few moments later I heard the dull shuffle of sandals on the hot stone. I didn't want to turn around, although I felt the shadow getting closer with every step. I tried to run. I couldn't. Suddenly I stopped short. Before I could defend myself, I felt the point of a knife in my back, and a sweet voice:

"Don't move, mister, or I'll stick it in."

Without turning, I asked:

"What do you want?"

"Your eyes, mister," answered the soft, almost painful voice.

"My eyes? What do you want with my eyes? Look, I've got some money. Not much, but it's something. I'll give you everything I have if you let me go. Don't kill me."

"Don't be afraid, mister. I won't kill you. I'm only going to take your eyes."

"But why do you want my eyes?" I asked again.

"My girlfriend has this whim. She wants a bouquet of blue eyes. And around here they're hard to find."

"My eyes won't help you. They're brown, not blue."

"Don't try to fool me, mister. I know very well that yours are blue."

"Don't take the eyes of a fellow-man. I'll give you something else."

"Don't play saint with me," he said harshly. "Turn around."

I turned. He was small and fragile. His palm sombrero covered half his face. In his right hand he held a country machete that shone in the moonlight.

"Let me see your face." I struck a match and put it close to my face. The brightness made me squint. He opened my eyelids with a firm hand. He couldn't see very well. Standing on tiptoe, he stared at me intensely. The flame burned my finger. I dropped it. A silent moment passed.

"Are you convinced now? They're not blue."

"Pretty clever, aren't you?" he answered. "Let's see. Light another one."

I struck another match, and put it near my eyes. Grabbing my sleeve, he ordered:

"Kneel down." I knelt. With one hand he grabbed me by the hair, pulling my head back. He bent over me, curious and tense, while his machete slowly dropped until it grazed my eyelids. I closed my eyes.

"Keep them open," he ordered. I opened my eyes. The flame burned my lashes. All of a sudden he let me go.

"All right, they're not blue. Beat it."

He vanished. I leaned against the wall, my head in my hands. I pulled myself together. Stumbling, falling, trying to get up again. I ran for an hour through the deserted town. When I got to the plaza, I saw the owner of the boardinghouse, still sitting in the front of the door. I went in without saying a word. The next day I left town.

Octavio Paz

An Unpleasant Reminder

Last summer, or perhaps it was only the other day - I find it so difficult to keep count of time now - I had a very disagreeable experience.

The day was ill-omened from the beginning; one of those unlucky days when every little detail seems to go wrong and one finds oneself engaged in a perpetual and infuriating strife with inanimate objects. How truly fiendish the sub-human world can be on these occasions! How every atom, every cell, every molecule, seems to be leagued in a maddening conspiracy against the unfortunate being who has incurred its obscure displeasure! This time, to make matters worse, the weather itself had decided to join in the fray. The sky was covered with a dull gray lid of cloud, the mountains had turned sour prussian blue, swarms of mosquitoes infested the shores of the lake. It was one of those sunless days that are infinitely more depressing than the bleakest winter weather; days when the whole atmosphere seems stale, and the world feels like a dustbin full of cold battered tins and fish scales and decayed cabbage stalks.

Of course, I was behindhand with everything all day long. I had to race through my changing for the game of tennis I had arranged to play in the afternoon, and as it was I was about ten minutes late. The other players had arrived and were having some practice shots as they waited for me. I was annoyed to see that they had chosen the middle court which is the one I like least of the three available for our use. When I asked why they had not taken the upper one, which is far the best, they replied that it had already been reserved for some official people. Then I suggested going to the lower court; but they grumbled and said that it was damp on account of the over-hanging trees. As there was no sun, I could not advance the principal objection to the middle court, which is that it lies the wrong way for the afternoon light. There was nothing for it but to begin playing.

The next irritating occurrence was that instead of keeping to my usual partner, David Post, it was for some reason decided that I should play with a man named Müller whom I hardly knew and who turned out to be a very inferior player. He was a bad loser as well, for as soon as it became clear that our opponents were too strong for us, he lost all interest in the game and behaved in a thoroughly unsporting manner. He was continually nodding and smiling to the people who stopped to watch us, paying far more attention to the onlookers than to the game. At other times, while the rest of us were collecting the balls or I was receiving the service, he would move away and stare at the main road which runs near, watching the cars as if he expected the arrival of someone he knew. In the end it became almost impossible to keep him on the court at all; he was always wandering off and having to be recalled by our indignant shouts. It seemed futile to continue the game in these circumstances, and at the end of the first set we abandoned play by mutual consent.

You can imagine that I was not in a particularly good mood when I got back to my room. Besides being in a state of nervous irritation I was hot and tired, and my chief object was to have a bath and change into fresh clothes as soon as possible. So I was not at all pleased to find a complete stranger waiting for me to whom I should have to attend before I did anything else.

She was a young woman of about my own age, quite attractive in a rather hard way, and neatly dressed in a tan linen suit, white shoes, and a hat with a white feather. She spoke well, but with a slight accent that I couldn't quite place: afterwards I came to the conclusion that she was a colonial of some sort.

As politely as I could I invited her to sit down and asked what I could do for her. She refused the chair, and, instead of giving a straightforward answer, spoke evasively, touching the racket which I still held in my hand, and making some inquiry about the strings. It seemed quite preposterous to me in the state I was in then to find myself involved with an unknown woman in an aimless discussion of the merits of different makes of rackets, and I'm afraid I closed the subject rather abruptly and asked her point-blank to state her business.

But then she looked at me in such a peculiar way, saying in quite a different voice, "You know, I'm really sorry I have to give you this," and I saw that she was holding out a box towards me, just an ordinary small, round, black pillbox that might have come from any druggist. And all at once I felt frightened and wished we could return to the conversation about the tennis rackets. But there was no going back.

I'm not sure now whether she told me in so many words or whether I simply deduced that the judgment which I had awaited for so long had at last been passed upon me and that this was the end. I remember - of all things! - feeling a little aggrieved because the sentence was conveyed to me in such a casual, unostentatious way, almost as if it were a commonplace event. I opened the box and saw the four white pellets inside.

"Now?" I asked. And I found that I was looking at my visitor with altered eyes, seeing her as an official messenger whose words had acquired a fatal portentousness.

She nodded without speaking. There was a pause. "The sooner the better," she said. I could feel the perspiration, still damp on me from the game, turning cold as ice.

"But at least I must have a bath first!" I cried out in a frantic way, clutching the clammy neck of my tennis shirt. "I can't stay like this - it's indecent - undignified!"

She told me that would be allowed as a special concession.

Into the bathroom I went like a doomed person, and turned on the taps. I don't remember anything about the bath; I suppose I must have washed and dried myself mechanically and put on my mauve silk dressing gown with the blue sash. Perhaps I even combed my hair and powdered my face. All I remember is the little black box confronting me all the time from the shelf over the basin where I had put it down.

At last I brought myself to the point of opening it and holding the four pills in the palm of my hand; I lifted them to my mouth. And then the most ridiculous contretemps occurred - there was no drinking glass in the bathroom. It must have got broken: or else the maid must have taken it away and forgotten to bring it back. What was I to do? I couldn't swallow even four such small pellets without a drink, and I couldn't endure any further delay. In despair I filled the soapdish with water and swallowed them down somehow. I hadn't even waited to wash out the slimy layer of soap at the bottom and the taste nearly made me sick. For several times I stood retching and choking and clinging to the edge of the basin. Then I sat down on the stool. I waited with my heart beating as violently as a hammer in my throat. I waited; and nothing happened, absolutely nothing whatever. I didn't even feel drowsy or faint.

But it was not till I got back to the other room and found my visitor gone that I realized that the whole episode had been a cruel hoax, just a reminder of what is in store for me.

Anna Kavan

A Story to Finish

It was a night in London in the late autumn of 1940. A bomb came whistling down, piercing the racket of the guns, and a man, a small shadowy figure, darted like a lizard into an already ruined house and flung himself down behind a pile of debris. He was none too soon, for the next instant the bomb exploded with a noise like the Day of Judgement less than a hundred yards away. He was quite unhurt, however, and it was only a few seconds before his ear drums began to work again and he realised that the objects which had spattered him all over were merely chips of brick and mortar.

Gilbert Moss, for that was his name, sat up and brushed some of the dust and plaster off his raincoat, after which he began mechanically feeling in his pockets for a cigarette. He noticed without surprise or even much interest that a dead man was lying face upwards a yard or two away from him. It did not seem to matter, either, that almost within touching distance some fallen beams or floor joists were burning fitfully. The whole house would be on fire before long, but in the mean time it gave a certain amount of protection.

Outside the barking of the guns rose and fell, sometimes bursting forth into an ear-splitting volley as a near-by battery came into action. This was the third time tonight that Gilbert had had to fling himself down to dodge a bomb, and on the second occasion he had had a small adventure, or what would have seemed an adventure in normal times. Caught by the blitz a long way from his own quarter of the town, he had struggled homewards through such a nightmare or gunfire, bomb flashes, falling shrapnel, burning houses and racing clanging fire engines as made him wonder whether the whole of humanity had not gone mad together. Under the rosy sky one had the impression that all London was burning. He had been passing down a side street he did not know when he heard a cry and saw a woman gesticulating to him from beside a demolished house. He hurried across to her. She was wearing blue overalls - curiously enough that was all he ever noticed about her - and a little boy of four or five, with a terrified face, was clutching at her leg. The woman cried out to him that there was a man under the wreckage and no rescue squad was near. With her help he had dug into the dusty pile of rubble, pushing and pulling at lumps of brick and mortar, splinters of glass, panels of smashed doors and fragments of furniture, and sure enough, within five minutes they had uncovered the body of a man, whitened to the eyes with plaster but conscious and almost unhurt. Gilbert never discovered whether the man was the woman's husband or father, or merely a stranger. They had just helped him out on to the pavement when there was the whistle of another bomb. Immediately one thought had filled Gilbert's mind to the exclusion or all others - the child. He had swiftly grabbed the little boy, laid him flat on the pavement and covered him with his own body against the moment when the bomb would burst. However, it was a delayed-action bomb and no roar followed the whistle. As he got up the woman had suddenly flung her arms round his neck and given him a kiss that tasted of plaster. And then he had gone on, promising to inform the next warden he met about the injured man. But as it happened he had not met any warden, and there the incident ended.

That was half an hour ago and Gilbert had already almost forgotten it. On a night like this nothing seemed remarkable. Since entering his new refuge he had hardly given a second glance to the dead man lying beside him. The pile of smouldering beams sent out little spurts of flame which illumined Gilbert and the wreckage of various pieces of furniture. He was a tall, smallish man in his middle thirties, with greying hair and a worn, sharp-featured, discoloured face. It had a sour expression which at most times was accentuated by a cigarette dangling from the lower lip. With his shabby raincoat and black felt hat he might have been an unsuccessful actor or journalist, a publisher's tout, a political agent or possibly some kind of hanger on of a lawyer's office. He could find no matches in his pockets and was considering lighting his cigarette from one of the burning beams when an A.R.P. [Air Raid Precautions] warden in overalls and gumboots threaded his way through from the back of the ruined house, flashing his torch from side to side.

"You O.K., chum?"

"I'm O.K." said Gilbert.

The warden waited for the echo of a gun to die away before speaking again. He flashed his torch briefly onto the prostrate man but seemed too preoccupied to examine him.

"This poor devil's done for," he said. "We got a packet tonight, all right. I'd better report him. They'll pick him up in the morning, I s'pose."

"No use wasting an ambulance," agreed Gilbert.

The A.R.P. man had just disappeared when the burning beams burst into bright flame and the room was almost as bright as day. Gilbert glanced again at the dead man lying at his side, and as he did so his heart gave a violent, painful leap. It was the figure of a rather handsome man of his own age, the face calm and undamaged, the eyes closed. In the better light, however, Gilbert had noticed two things. In the first place it was not a stranger but a man he knew very well - or had once known very well, rather. In the second place the man was not dead, nor anywhere near it. He was merely unconscious, perhaps stunned by a falling beam.

A change had come over Gilbert's face the instant that the shock of recognition passed. It became very intent, with the ghost of a smile. The expression he wore was not a wicked expression, exactly - rather the expression of a man faced with an overwhelming temptation, an opportunity too good to be missed.

Suddenly he sprang to his feet and began looking for something which he knew he would have no difficulty in finding. In a moment he had got it. It was a heavy billet of wood, part of a broken floor joist, four feet long and tapering at one end to form a natural handle. He tested its weight and then, carefully measuring his distance from the unconscious man on the floor, gripped it with both hands and swung it aloft. Outside the guns were roaring again. Gilbert did not immediately deliver his blow. The man's head was not quite in the right position, and with the toe of his boot Gilbert pushed a few flakes of plaster under the head, raising it slightly. Then he took a fresh grip on his billet of wood and swung it aloft again. It was a heavy, formidable club. He had only to bring it down once and the skull would break like an egg.

At this moment he felt no fear, any more than he felt compunction. Curiously enough the racket of the guns upheld him. He was utterly alone in the burning town. He did not even need to reflect that on a night like this any death whatever would be attributed to the German bombs. He knew instinctively that in the middle of this nightmare you could do what you liked and nobody would have time to notice. Nevertheless the moment in which he had paused had temporarily saved the unconscious man's life. Gilbert lowered his club and leaned on it, as on a walking stick. He wanted, not exactly to think things over, but to recapture a certain memory, a certain feeling. It is not much use killing your enemy unless in the moment of striking him you remember just what he has done to you. It was not that he had faltered in his intention of killing this man. There was no question that he was going to kill him. But before doing so he wanted, in a sense, to remember *why* he was doing so. There was plenty of time, and complete safety. In the morning his enemy's body would only be one air-raid casualty among hundreds of others.

He leaned his club against a pile of wreckage and again took his unlighted cigarette from his pocket. He still could not find any matches. A thought striking him, he knelt down and felt in the unconscious man's pockets till he came on a slim gold cigarette-lighter. He lit his cigarette and put the lighter back, rather reluctantly. The initials on it were C.J.K.C., he noted. He had known this man as Charles Coburn, the Honourable Charles Coburn. Doubtless he was a lord by this time, though Gilbert could not remember the name of the title he was heir to. It was curious, but the excellent cloth of the man's waistcoat, and the expensive feel of the slender gold lighter, partly brought back the memory that he was looking for. They both felt like money. Gilbert had known Charles Coburn as a very rich young man, horribly elegant and superior, and rather cultured as they used to call it in the nineteen-twenties. With not many exceptions Gilbert hated all rich people - though that in itself was not a motive for killing anybody, or course.

He sat down again and drew the cigarette smoke deep into his lungs. The chorus of the guns stopped for nearly two minutes, then opened up again. It was so hard to remember - not the *fact*, of course, but the social atmosphere in which such things could happen. He remembered in great detail the outrageous, mean injury which this man had done him; what he did not remember so well were his own feelings at the time, the weakness and snobbishness which had made it possible for such a petty humiliating disaster to happen to him. To remember that he had to remember the England of the nineteen-twenties, the old, snobbish, money-ruled England which was fast disappearing before the bombers and the income-tax came to finish it off. For a moment it eluded him, then suddenly it came back to him in a vision of a Mayfair street one summer morning - the flowers in the window boxes, a water cart laying the dust, a footman in a striped waistcoat opening a door. He could not remember when he had seen that particular street, or whether he had ever seen it. Perhaps it was only a symbolic street. But there it was, in the smell of pink geraniums and newly drenched dust - fashionable London with its clubs and its gunsmiths and its footmen in striped waistcoats, the London of before the deluge, when money ruled the world and creatures like Charles Coburn were all-powerful because of their money.

Gilbert sprang to his feet again. He had no more doubts now. He did not merely know in an intellectual sense that he hated the man lying at his feet, he knew just why and how he hated him. Nor did it seem to him a barbarous thing to kill your enemy when you have him at your mercy; on the contrary, it seemed to him natural. As though encouraging him, the guns rose once again to an unbroken, rolling roar, like thunder. With an expression on his face much more purposeful than before he once more measured his distance, gripped his club firmly in both hands and swung it above his head, ready for a blow that would settle his enemy once and for all.

George Orwell

What a Beauty!

Theo van den Boogaard

ACTIVITIES

Mini- and Micro-stories

This section of the book contains mini-stories; some of them are so short that they might be called micro-stories. Because this is a book, the stories are written down. But you have only to listen to people talking around you to realise how many of these mini-stories we tell and listen to in the course of a day.

Conversation is full of stories, ranging from reports ("She said to me ... and so I said to her ..."), short anecdotes and incidents from personal life ("He was just telling me what I'd done wrong when he fell straight off his chair!"), through to full, blow by blow accounts of what happened (e.g. in the match) and the teller's part in it. Many writers draw on these snippets of stories as the basis for their work. Their notebooks are full of snatches overheard on buses ("Well, the doctor said to me: 'They'll never be any use to you again, not as feet.'").

- You can have a lot of fun with micro-stories. Record a fifteen-minute chat between a group of people at home or at school and analyse it to find out how many mini-stories are told and why. What is the shortest of the stories told?
- Keep a notebook for a week in which you collect the possible germs of stories and select four to develop.
- Run a competition for the most tantalising phrases overheard on the bus or train and turn these into a set of micro-stories.

A Better Place
Brett Lovell

Saturday Shopping
Diana Rigg

A Cautionary Tale of the Calorific Pitfalls on the Road to True Love
Penny Maplestone

These micro-stories are from a collection called *The Book of Mini-Sagas II*. Each 'saga' is only 50 words long.

- Micro-stories are fun to try. A good approach is to write them with a partner. Give each other a theme, then each of you takes 10 minutes to write the story in 50 words. Then together you make up titles for your stories. The title is an important part of a story of this length.
- Another approach is to condense the story of a novel or film you have enjoyed into 50 words.
- You will notice that these micro-stories are set out in an unconventional way for prose writing. What do you think they gain from this?

Winnie and Walter
Anonymous

This amazing 450-word story, in which every word begins with 'w' comes from *Everybody's Scrapbook of Curious Facts*, published one hundred years ago.

- What happens in the story?
- Now choose a letter and try your own story. See how far you can get. (It might be easier in pairs!)

Freedom to Breathe
Alexander Solzhenitsyn

Alexander Solzhenitsyn was born in the Soviet Union in 1918. He was imprisoned in Arctic labour camps for eight years, and was released only when the Soviet leader, Stalin, died in 1953. He was awarded the Nobel Prize for Literature in 1970.

- It has rained. A man stands breathing deeply under an apple tree in blossom. This seems to be a very small happening, but is an immensely significant experience for the writer.
- What happens to this piece if you put its four paragraphs into a different order? Is it more or less effective?
- Find other pieces in this book which describe freedom. How do they differ? Which do you prefer and why?
- Try writing a short piece like this in which you describe an occasion when you felt suddenly free. You could do this either from your own experience or as a piece of fiction. Perhaps you could use real events in the world as a background to your story.

Which of these are stories?
Various authors

- Here are 11 short texts. Which of them are complete stories?
- Read the texts on your own first, then discuss in small groups which pieces you think are stories and which are not. Of those that are not, what are they? How would you identify them?
- Here are the sources of the 11 short texts. See if you can match each source to the text. (The answers are on page 106).

1. The blurb of Louise Erdrich's collection of short stories, *Love Medicine*.

2. The 'argument' (i.e. summary at the beginning of a chapter) from Chapter IV of 'A Voyage to Brobdingnag' in *Gulliver's Travels*.

3. A poem by Ken Jones. Would it be a story if you left out the last line?

4. A joke.

5. From *The Vikings* by Robin Place - a book of information sold to tourists at the Jorvik Centre, York.

6. The beginning of the Doris Lessing space fiction novel, *Shikasta*.

7. A poem by Wordsworth from *Lyrical Ballads*.

8. Almost the complete text of *The Tiger and the Tortoise* by Wang Janrong. The missing last sentence is, 'The tortoise agrees but upon reaching midstream pushes the helpless tiger into the river.'

9. A true story, told by Richard Andrews.

10. Part of Billy Pilgrim's dream from Kurt Vonnegut's *Slaughterhouse Five*.

11. A list - but is it a story?

Notation, Litotes, Interjections and **Official Letter**
Raymond Queneau

These four pieces are all retellings of the same incident, each in a different style. In 'Notation' we have the incident as the writer might have jotted it down in a notebook. 'Interjections' tells the story as a soundtrack, through odd words and grunts. 'Litotes' tells the basic incident without drama. ('Litotes' means understatement to create an effect.)

- Go on with the sequence. Write an official letter about the incident, or draw a cartoon strip. Try writing about the incident in a dialect you know, or as a poem. Queneau manages 129 different ways!
- Make yourselves into groups of four. Each of you in turn contributes a brief incident, something you have seen in passing or in which you have been briefly involved. Then decide on four styles you would like to use to write about the incidents. You might like to use the same ones as Queneau, or you could try writing in the style of a song writer, a writer of ghost stories, a Radio One presenter or a magazine journalist. Or you could invent some styles of your own.

The Full Bus
John Cage

- Tell the story of the full bus from the viewpoint of someone who was there. You could choose the conductress, the policeman, or the person who really was the last to get on the bus but would not say so.
- In groups, improvise the conversations that took place on the bus whilst the conductress, the driver and the inspector had gone to find a police officer.
- Write a short statement saying what you think this story is about. Compare your statement with those of others in your group. Do you agree or not? Put your statements together to form a majority joint account of what was going on. Remember to record any disagreements or minority views.

On Discovery
Maxine Hong Kingston

Maxine Hong Kingston was born in California in 1940, the daughter of Chinese immigrants. Her books deal with what it is like to inherit Chinese memories and ways of behaving from her parents whilst living in America where so many different nationalities have made their home. 'On Discovery' is taken from *China Men*. The author's other book is *The Woman Warrior: memoirs of a girlhood among ghosts*.

- 'On Discovery' is a story with a purpose; it tells us how life used to be for some women in China, and it explores what those experiences must have felt like. How does the author feel about them?
- Tang Ao sets out to discover the Gold Mountain, America. What is discovered in the story, by Tang Ao and also by you, the reader? Write these discoveries down as a set of statements. Then see how they compare with other people's 'statements of discovery'.
- Find out about the practice of footbinding in China; why it was performed, when it came to an end and why. Maxine Hong Kingston has written about this in *The Woman Warrior*.

Activities - Mini- and Micro-stories   105

On Fathers
Maxine Hong Kingston

- Imagine another case of mistaken identity, and write a story of about this length; or imagine that the first man *did* play along with the idea that he was the father of the children. Continue the story in a different way from, 'The littlest ones hugged his legs for a ride on his shoes.'
- Why do you think that this story is called 'On Fathers' - as though it was about fathers in general?

The Captive
Jorge Luis Borges

Borges died recently. He lived in Buenos Aires in Argentina, and he was blind for most of his writing life. Borges retells an old story, one that is part of a stock of stories told in any frontier town. It is a very condensed story, which could be expanded in many ways.

- Imagine you had decided to turn this story into a film. Where would you set it? How would the film start and at what point in the story would you finish it? What sort of ending would it have? What would the film be about? Working in pairs, plot out the main scenes in the film. You could spend about half an hour on this or you could take longer and produce a draft synopsis for shooting. Look out for other stories or films in which children are snatched from their homes and brought up by people of another culture, or by animals, as in Kipling's 'Mowgli' stories.
- When Borges has told the story he tells us the questions the story raises for him. Under the heading 'I would like to know' write down two questions of your own. See what answers your partner can provide.
- Answer Borges' questions - or your own or your partner's - in a continuation of this story, told from the boy's point of view.

Cat in the Rain
Ernest Hemingway

Ernest Hemingway was born in 1899 in Chicago. He was badly wounded in Italy in the First World War, and visited Spain during the Civil War. Hemingway was a newspaper reporter and war correspondent before becoming a novelist and short story writer. He discovered a tough, peculiarly American style of writing. His books include *A Farewell to Arms*, *For Whom the Bell Tolls*, and *The Old Man and the Sea*. Hemingway died in Cuba in 1961.

This story reads as if it were based on an incident in real life. It is raining on holiday.

- Hemingway's style, influenced by his time as a journalist, has been described as 'verbal photography of action'. Imagine you have been asked to rework 'Cat in the Rain' as a photo story. Pick out from Hemingway's description the photographs you would need to use. How many photo-frames would you need to tell the story and what would each show?
- 'Cat in the Rain' is told from the viewpoint of the American wife. But what does the husband think about the incident? What does the maid say to her family when she gets home after work that day? Choose your characters and then improvise a scene in which the story is told again. You could choose the husband, back from holiday, telling it to friends,

106 Activities - *Tales which Teach*

or the time when the padrone tells the maid what the American Signora requires. Or you could finish the story from the wife's point of view.
- Would this story be better or worse if the first paragraph was left out? Why do you think we are told the husband's name but we do not know the name of the wife? Would it make any difference if we did know her name?

The answers to 'Which of these are stories', (page 103) are:
I-6, II-3, III-11, IV-1, V-10, VI-2, VII-7, VIII-9, IX-8, X-4, XI-5.

Tales which Teach

The group of stories in this section are all stories with a purpose: they set out to teach. They include creation myths, stories which explain how the world began. They also include a number of fables. Fables are stories with a moral. Children are often the target audience for fables in which talking animals are the main characters. But fables can have other, more political, purposes as you will see here.
   Some of these stories are ancient. Others, written more recently, draw on the old forms to convey their message. All these stories are short. They could all be told orally as well as read on the page.

You might explore the possibilities of these myths, fables and anecdotes in the following ways:
- Collect further examples of animal fables. If you have younger brothers and sisters you can find out which fables they most enjoy and how the fables are illustrated.
- Try making up some modern fables, as Pitika Ntuli does in 'A Story of Our Times'.
- Invent a wise person, like Brecht's Mr Keuner, and invent some anecdotes for her or him to tell. The stories can illustrate some of the principles you would like people to live by. Alternatively, you could build these anecdotes round some of the old proverbs:
'A bird in the hand is worth two in the bush'
'A stitch in time saves nine'.
You could then make a recording of these anecdotes.

The Great Manito
Delaware Indians

The story of the Great Manito, the God of the Delaware Indians and how he created the world.

- The story is in twenty-four sections, each of which consists of a single sentence. However, the sections have been jumbled up. Recreate the story, putting the sections in what you think is the right order.

- Each section has an illustration that goes with it. Now write your own creation myth, using simple images like these to go with your story. You can set it out in cartoon-like boxes on a page, or on a long strip of paper, like a scroll.

Why the Sky is Far Away
Bini people
***from the* Popul Vuh**
Mayan people

'Why the Sky is Far Away' is a creation-myth of the Bini people, a tribe in Nigeria.

The 'Popul Vuh' is a creation story of the Mayan people of Central America.
    Creation myths are handed down from generation to generation. It is only comparatively recently that they have been collected and printed on the page. They are meant to be told aloud.

- Choose a creation myth which particularly catches your attention and try retelling it to your group. (Don't write it down first.) You could try telling it in your local dialect, or in the special language of school. There is a Yorkshire version of God's creation of the world which begin, 'First on, there were nobbut God'.
- What other creation myths do you know? Did you read about them or were they told to you?
- See how many other stories you can collect, including the Bible story of God's creation of the world.
- Creation myths make good subjects for illustration. Tell one of these stories in a series of simple diagrams or pictures, with captions. Use whatever materials you think most suitable. No one really knows how the world was created. Make up your own account, and be prepared to justify it.

A Story of Our Times
Pitika Ntuli

This is a story from modern Africa. It is a story with a purpose, told in the style of traditional stories.

- 'A Story of Our Times' contains many references to time. What is the time span of the incidents described in the story? Try retelling the story, leaving out the references to time. What difference does this make to the story's effect?
- Try writing a story in this style about an injustice which concerns you at the moment.

Dog Digs to China
Linda Combi

- Collect as many strip cartoons as you can find in newspapers, magazines and comics. Group them according to the number of boxes they use. Display them in groups on the walls of the classroom.
- Create your own strip cartoon, and display it alongside those from published sources.

Activities - Tales which Teach

The North Wind and the Sun
La Fontaine

The Chicks' Nest
Wu Guangxiao

The Two Clay Men
Du Li

The first of these three fables was written in France about three hundred years ago. The other two fables are from present-day China.

Fables illustrate simple, homely truths. Often they warn us against falling prey to common human weaknesses such as pride, envy, greed or flattery. Many fables take animals as the main characters.

- Working in pairs or small groups, look at what these three fables have in common and how they are different. Then rank them in order of preference. Be prepared to justify your choice.
- Working in pairs, each of you could devise a moral for today. Then give it to your partner who writes a fable to illustrate it. Or try taking a traditional story such as the 'Three Little Pigs' and retelling it to illustrate a moral for today.

Two Feminist Fables
Suniti Namjoshi

The Giantess

Suniti Namjoshi was born in India in 1941 and now works in Canada. These stories appear in Hermione Lee's collection, *The Secret Self 2*.

- Carry on the fable. It is exactly one year since the giantess crossed the mountain. What has happened in that year? Improvise the conversation between the three men who tried to persuade her to stay.

Of Cats and Bells

- There are seven mice in the fable, each with its own character. What other ways are there of belling the cat? In groups of three, decide three additional characters to add to Little Mouse, Big Mouse and Heroic Mouse and continue the debate about how to bell the cat.

Anecdotes of Mr Keuner: Good Turns
Bertolt Brecht

Brecht was a German poet, playwright and teacher. Persecuted by the Nazis for his communism, he fled to the USA in the 1930s, returning to East Berlin after the Second World War to found a theatre. 'Good Turns' is one of the anecdotes of Brecht's fictional wise man, Herr Keuner, in the book *Tales from the Calendar*.

- Mr Keuner is a wise man, a teacher. Imagine what might have happened to his group of friends which has prompted him to tell them this story. Can you test the way the old Arab solved the problem?
- Improvise a short scene in which friends are having trouble with a problem and a solution is offered by someone like Mr Keuner. The problem is solved. Write another anecdote - or series of anecdotes - for Mr Keuner, to illustrate how friends should behave.

The Woodcutter's Son
Fred Manley

This story was told by Fred Manley at a school in East London. Fred is a Romany and was born in Spain during the Civil War in the 1930s. He now lives in London.

- Listen to this story being read to you. You don't need to follow the text as you listen. When you have heard and enjoyed the story, look at the text. What do you notice about it that is distinctively speech-like rather than literary?
- Make a list of as many features as you can identify that are more common in told stories than in written ones. Compare notes with a partner, then with the class as a whole.
- Read the introduction to the next section of this book, 'The Voice on the Page' (see below).

Images towards Story-writing
Linda Combi

Linda Combi is an illustrator who lives in York.

- The images on page 36 have been provided for you to write stories from. Select at least three of the images and make notes on a story that will connect the images. You can put the images in whatever order you like. You might find that your notes cover the whole story, or that you are writing or composing just the beginning, and that you don't yet know where you will end.
- Then either tell or write the story.
- When you have told or written the complete story, tell or write that same story in a different order. It will help you if you refer back to your original sequence of images. How many different ways are there of telling your same story?
- In pairs, read your stories to each other; and then hear a few in the class as a whole.
- Expand and contract stories. It can be fun to condense a novel or film which you have enjoyed into 100 words (or even 50 words). Or you can take one of the micro-stories in this book and build it up into a longer story, or block out the story as the main scenes for a film.

The Voice on the Page

All the texts in this section are close to the speaking voice: from Linda Haas' recollection of a friend through the song, interview and sketch, to the autobiographical extract, the memories of childhood and the radio broadcast. Many of the pieces have the rough energy of speech, as well as the immediacy that makes you feel that speaker is close to you. They are dramatic, authentic and compelling.

There is much that you can explore about spoken narratives. Here are a few general ideas:

- **Telling stories**: first, think about a story you could tell. It could either be an anecdote about some experience you've had - some close shave or coincidence, for instance - or it could be a fully fledged ghost story, a long joke or a folk-tale that you have heard. Another idea is to retell a written story or novel that you have read. Rehearse it two or three times until you are sure you can remember the basic outline of it.

  Tell this story in a group of four or five of your friends at school, and record all your various stories on tape.

  You might like to select the best of these stories for retelling or playing to the class as a whole.

  It might also be interesting to transcribe (write down) the actual words on the tape, so that you have a written record of your told story.

- *Comparing told and written stories*: take the story you told and write it as though you were writing the story without any regard to the spoken version. Then compare the written and spoken (transcribed) versions of the same stories. What differences do you notice? Make a list of them and then compare notes with others in your group.

- *Listen to people talking*, and, if possible, record them. When do they use stories? How do they tell them? How do people stand - say, on a street corner or on a doorstep - when they are exchanging stories? How do the stories sound in relation the rest of their speech? Is it possible to say where the stories begin and end?

- *Ask your parents and grandparents*, or other members of your family about the stories you enjoyed listening to as a child. Did you enjoy the same story again and again? Did you have several favourite stories? Are there stories about you when you were a child that the grown-ups like to tell again and again?

- *Is there a storyteller in the community* who could be invited to school to tell some tales?

Timelines
Gabriel Swartland and *Amy Strickland*

The idea of a personal timeline that goes beyond the personal was developed by teachers on the New York City Writing Project.

- Map out your own timeline. Include the columns as set out in the examples by the two writers, both of whom were students in school at the time they composed their timelines. Fill in as much as you can.
- Do you see any connections between local and world events and your own life? Do the sequences surprise you in any way?
- Use the completed timeline as the basis for a piece of reflective autobiographical writing.

Activities - The Voice on the Page   111

'Everyone thought he was cool and tough ...'
Linda Haas

This piece was originally written as an assignment for an English class in the USA. The author is offering the portrait of her friend to an interviewer, from memory: 'Just a guy I grew up with, Spanish. He's a nice person, but he has to be in a gang.' It is from Studs Terkel's collection, *American Dreams*.

- Interview each other about people you know well. Try to build up portraits in words. Then transcribe the interview, or make notes from it to act as the basis of a written portrait.
- Linda Haas seems to be accepted by the gangs, and yet she is outside them. Imagine that you are Linda and tell more stories about observing gang life from the outside.
- Discuss the following statements in small groups:
  - it is better to be outside a gang than inside it
  - gangs are for weak people who can't stand on their own two feet
  - gangs don't exist anymore
  - there is always a leader in a gang
  - most gangs cause trouble.

The Projectile
Raymond Carver

This poem is in the collection *In a Marine Light*, published in 1988, the year Carver died. He lived in Washington State in the north-west of the USA. He also wrote short stories which are collected in *The Stories of Raymond Carver*.

- Cover up the following parts of the poem:
  - the first eight lines,
  - the sentence 'See it speeding ... the dread fascination of it',
  - the last two lines.
- Now discuss the following statements:
  - Excluding these parts makes no difference to the poem's effect.
  - The poem is better if you include these parts.
  - One of the covered-up parts is more important than the others.
- Write out part of this poem in prose: what difference does it make to have it set out as a poem? Choose some line-endings in the poem and give reasons to explain why Carver started a new line at these points.
- Read the poem to a friend who hasn't seen or heard the whole poem. Stop in one or two places and ask your friend to predict what is going to happen in the rest of the story. (You might want to stop in several places.)
- 'A room that for a minute something else entered.' In a group of five or six people, try an improvisation in which a conversation between two characters is 'interrupted' by a minute or so's reenactment of a memory of one of the characters. Two group members are the characters. The rest of the group act out the memory recalled by one character.
- 'The guy who threw it ... got lost/in his life, same as I got lost in

mine.' Write a letter to Raymond Carver from this man, in which he describes his life. Perhaps he did remember 'that stupid car sliding/down the road'?

Testament of a Little Doffer
Elizabeth Bentley

This evidence was given by a millhand to parliamentary commissioners who were investigating the employment of children in factories in Britain at the beginning of the nineteenth century. It is collected in *The Faber Book of Reportage*, (ed.) John Carey.

- Find out what you can about the conditions in mills and other factories for children at the start of the Industrial Revolution. Present this information as a report, either written or oral.
- Imagine that you were either a child worker or an 'overlooker' in a nineteenth-century factory. Write a poem or prose account of your feelings at work.
- Describe the scene during the parliamentary commissioners' questioning of Elizabeth as if you had been present. You could write this as a letter, or as an entry in a journal.
- What would the commissioners' report be like after interviews such as this one? You might like to enact further interviews of this kind (once you have gathered more evidence), and then write the report they might have written for parliament.

'I have to be a waitress ...'
Dolores Dante

From Studs Terkel's *Working*: accounts based on interviews with people in America about their work.

- Read this (aloud) to yourself. Try to capture the voice and the person behind the words.
- Now imagine you were producing a radio programme on people's experience of work and you wanted to include this account by Dolores Dante. You only have space for something half this length. How could you cut this without losing the character or continuity of it? Take a pencil and make a note of which parts you would use and which you would cut. Record the edited version on tape.
- Once you have practised interviewing on your school friends and/or parents, interview someone you don't know well. Make the focus of the interview the subject of work. You could choose someone who has a job you would like to do when you leave school or college; or you might choose someone for general interest's sake. Either transcribe or make notes from the recorded interview, then write up the account as a case study of this person's view of work. The class collection of case studies can be bound to form a book or magazine for others to read.

Family Snaps

These photographs were taken over a number of years of members of the same family.

Activities - The Voice on the Page   113

- In pairs, identify the two people who appear in all three photographs. Work out how old they are in each photograph, and when you think the photos were taken.
- Then look together at the family group shot. Give names to each of the people in the photograph and say how everyone is related (unless you think that some are friends of the family).
- Bring in a selection of photographs from your family's collection. Use them as a basis to write either an autobiographical account of how you have changed, or a biography of someone in your family.

John
John Best

Many of the texts in this section of the book are autobiographical. This extract comes from *Writing*, an anthology of writing from the Worker Writers and Community Publishers. The anthology is one of a series put together in Partington, Manchester, in 1974-75. The autobiographical accounts were either recorded, transcribed and worked up into prose, or written straight from memory.

- What questions would you ask John Best if you could? Perhaps you can note these and ask each other in small groups; any questions that remain unanswered could be asked of the whole class and the teacher.
- John Best mentions dreams, particularly striking events, ordinary memories and dates and places as well as **reflecting** on his childhood. Try to record your own recollections of childhood, aiming to make your writing as lively and clear as you can. You can experiment with the way you tell the story. It could be in any of the following patterns (or a combination of all of them):
    - chronologically
    - based purely on memory
    - using documents from your childhood such as photographs or letters
    - using the accounts of parents and others who knew you
    - backwards, from the present to the past
    - fictionalised, so that your own identity is disguised
    - in dialogue form as well as in continuous prose.

'I used to think babies ...'
Iris Bradford

This extract is from an oral history of working class youth called *Hooligans or Rebels*, by Stephen Humphries. The speaker is an old woman who is recalling her childhood.

- Your school may already have a connection with an old people's centre. If not, one way of establishing such a relationship is to ask if you can record old people talking about their memories. You could take in photographs of your town from earlier this century as a way of getting people started. Alternatively, you could get your own grandparents talking - if they live near you. You could make your own book, based on the recordings.

The Toilet
Gcina Mhlope

Gcina Mhlope is black South African. Her story is about how she became a writer and how the circumstances of her life in South Africa brought this about. The story is part of a collection called *Sometimes When It Rains* (ed.) Ann Oosthuisen.

- A feature of this piece of writing is that it contains a number of stories within it. Briefly note these stories. Try arranging the stories in a different order. What difference would this re-ordering make?
- The story contains many physical descriptions. Make a note of them, and discuss what effect these descriptions have on the story.
- There are several ways in which you could take work on this story forward. You could improvise the whispered row between the two sisters when the alarm goes off, or the scene at the clothing factory when the supervisor finds two dresses have been stolen. You could script the scene at the swimming pool when the sister's employer tells her friends about how she found Mholo sitting outside Irene's room, threatened by dogs. Or, moving away from the story, you could write about an occasion when you have been really frightened, trying to create the vividness of detail of this writer.

A Recollection
Frances Cornford

Cornford was a British poet born in 1886. This poem appears in *The Faber Book of Twentieth-Century Women's Poetry*. It originally appeared in *Collected Poems*.

- There are three states of mind or kinds of feeling presented here: the laughing and talking that took place at tea when the father's friend was alive; the 'sadness' that is expressed on his death; and the pride felt by the girl or young woman on knowing a person who has died.
- See if you can create a poem or story with three such 'states' in it: one event that happened in the past, and two different responses to it from different people (or within the same person).
- How old do you think the speaker in the poem is?

Blind Date
Bob Clarke

This comic strip is from *Mad* magazine.

- 'Two Sides to Every Story Dept.': imagine an event which is told from two very different points of view. It could be a blind date, as in this story, or it could be an accident, an account of why two people break off their relationship, a court case etc. You could 'tell' it in comic strip form, as an argument, in separate stories told to friends, as a play or in any other way you think appropriate or amusing.
- Collect several examples of comic strip stories from magazines, as well as serial cartoons like 'Doonesbury' or 'Peanuts'. You might like to make an exhibition of them, and/or take a survey to see who reads what in the school. Others in the class could analyse the various stories in terms of intended audience, number of frames, kinds of language used etc. There is scope for a whole-class project here, with groups working

Activities - This is How it Was   115

on different aspects of comic strip stories.
● If you have access to art materials, you could attempt to create your own comic strip story.

Learning to Stalk Muskrats
Annie Dillard

This extract is from Annie Dillard's book, *Pilgrim at Tinker Creek*, in which she reflects on her experiences living in the backwoods in the eastern part of the USA.

● Although this extract tells a story of two sightings of muskrats, it is primarily descriptive. While you probably will not be able to stalk or observe muskrats, you can use this passage as a model for the observation of some creature or person who does not know he or she is being observed. Once you have chosen your subject, you will have to find a place where you can make notes without being seen. Try to capture the distinctive features and movements of your subject (and of yourself as the observer), then write up the story of how you managed your observation, including the details you observed. If you find it difficult to set up, choose a subject that is easy to observe, like a pet or someone in your family!

Service Wash
Victoria Wood

This sketch appears in *Up to You, Porky*. It takes the form of a monologue by the 'old bag' in a launderette.

● Try to write one or two paragraphs that might have come from 'Service Wash'. Then get into groups and combine your paragraphs in different orders until you have a sequence that seems right. Read them out (in groups) around the class.
● Write your own sketch, in monologue (one person speaking) or dialogue, taking any character and any setting you like. (It might be a bus driver speaking from his cab, a taxi-driver, a school cleaner, a disillusioned headteacher....) Try to make it funny. Possible beginnings are 'When I was young ...', 'I can remember ...', 'You young'uns don't know you're born ...'.
● Photocopy this sketch, then cut it up into its paragraphs. How many different sequences can you make?

This is How it Was

This section contains many true stories; reports on 'how it was', or what happened. If there is an 'I' reporting what he or she saw and experienced, that 'I' is much more in the background than in the texts in the previous section, such as Dolores Dante's, 'I have to be a waitress'. Sometimes there is no 'I' in the stories at all, as in the newspaper article about the trial of the Puerto Rican bandit in 'True Stories'.

Furthermore - as you would expect if the writer is reporting something extraordinary - the scene of the event is often some way from home. Travel writing can be included here, whether it's travel to a church in your home town or a report on being in a different country.

Here are some general ideas for writing and speech of this kind, in addition to the specific ideas mentioned in relation to each text:

- *commentary*: try commentating (in speech) on some event, such as a school sports day or an event broadcast on television with the sound turned down.
- *reporting*: investigative reporting in your community and/or within the school can produce interesting 'stories' that you could write up for any magazine or newspaper you are working on.
- *travel writing*: 'What we did on our holidays' is a popular title for writing in school, especially for the first week in September! But travel writing can be much more exciting than the usual clichéd response to this title. It could be based on a journal of a trip, or be designed for others to read who are thinking of making the same journey as you. You can choose various styles and tones to make your writing interesting to read.

True Stories
Christopher Logue

'True Stories' is a regular column in the satirical magazine *Private Eye*, edited by Christopher Logue. Readers of the column send in cuttings from newspapers or other publications and are paid if their story is used.

- Rank the three stories in order of quality. Compare your order with others to see if you agree.
- Take any one of these micro-stories and expand it into a full-length short story. What kinds of elements will you need to add to achieve this?
- See if you can collect further micro-stories like these allegedly true ones. Where are they published?

'I was on a bus to Washington, D.C. ...'
Tobias Wolff

This is from a collection of very short stories called *Sudden Fiction*.

- '... What is it, what's going on here? Why can't I ever forget them? Tell me, for God's sake, but make it snappy - I'm tired, and the bus is picking up speed, and the lunatic beside me is getting ready to say something.' Write the answer to Tobias Wolff's questions as if you were sitting on the bus talking to him, and as if you knew all about the people he has seen.
- Photographs are one way of freezing moments like the one described. Collect some dramatic photographs from magazines and colour supplements. You can either use one picture, and imagine what went on before the photo was taken, and after it; who the people are

and what they are doing; or several pictures, and make connections between them. When you use more than one picture, you can experiment with the order until you get a story that satisfies you. Whichever way you approach this exercise, you can fictionalise the story if you wish.
- 'I was on a bus to Washington, D.C. ...' is a minute example of travel writing, in which things seen, felt or experienced can be recorded to entertain and enlighten others. You could try either remembering a particular journey you have taken and recording it in words (you might have a photographic or written record to jog your memory) or make a point of writing an account of a journey you are going to take in the near future. It doesn't have to be a boat trip up the Amazon to be interesting to write (or read!).

Solo Tackle
Ramon Figueroa

This piece was written in 1979 as part of a memory-writing workshop. The first passage shows Ramon's first attempt at recording something memorable from his past. This was read by three members of a group who responded with comments to questions set by Ramon. These questions were:
- Did I choose an interesting memory?
- What would you like to know more about?
- Should I leave out any details? Which ones?
- What part should I emphasize?
- Can you tell how I felt? If not, where should I put in my feelings?

Ramon rewrote the story in the light of the responses he received.

- Look at one passage alongside the other. List some of the changes Ramon has made to his first draft. Are they all improvements? Discuss your opinions in a small group.
- You might like to try the process of writing from memory as practised by Ramon. First, for up to five minutes, let one memory trigger off another and list them quickly on a sheet of paper. Don't stop to reflect on these memories or try to alter the course of the memories.
- Next, compare notes with a partner. Do you both have the same kind of memory chains? Take each other through the sequence of memories, explaining how each one came about.
- Draw a box around the area of the memory chain that you would most like to write about. This might be the memory or cluster of memories that is most important to you. Do any other items in the chain relate to this memory?
- Now write quickly - without worrying about spelling or other aspects of presentation - for about ten minutes on the subject you have chosen.
- Again form groups, and read what you have written so far to the other members of the group. At this point you can follow the procedure outlined above in the making of Ramon's story.

Travelling in a Comfortable Car
Bertolt Brecht

As well as being a dramatist and prose-writer, Brecht was a prolific poet.

- Write this poem out as prose: what difference does it make?
- '... we heard me say': the narrator of the poem (the 'I' of the third line from the end) who uses 'we' to tell the story, refers to him - or herself as if he (or she?) was someone else; as if his or her voice was disembodied. This is rather like having (at least) two voices going on in your head at the same time. Can you create a story in which the narrator or one of the characters has two 'voices'?
- What do you think causes the writer to be suddenly shocked when 'we had gone a long way'? See if you can describe what was on his mind.
- Imagine that instead of driving on, the car stops to pick up the 'ragged fellow at nightfall'. Continue the poem from line 4 onwards, either in poetic form or as a story.

The Fire of London and **A Prize-Fight**
Samuel Pepys

Pepys kept a diary during the middle of the seventeenth century, recording public as well as personal observations. It is written in code.

- If you don't already keep a diary, it is worth experimenting with one for a short period to see what kinds of things you do record. Entries do not have to be made every day; only when you feel you have something to say. There could well be more than one entry a day, and the individual entries might vary considerably in length.

Working from a Photograph
Pete Skingley

Photographs capture a particular moment in time. What *you* make of that moment may be different from what actually happened.

- In pairs, look at the photograph and suggest what you think has just happened, what is happening/being said now, and what will happen next. Give each of the figures in the photograph a name and a history. Discuss your suggestions with the class as a whole.
- Write a monologue from the point of view of one of the figures, telling her story.

Comparative Methods of Medicine
Ousama

Ingrafting the Small-pox
Lady Mary Wortley Montagu

Ousama, who lived in the twelfth century, was a Saracen and fought in the Crusades against the Christians. 'Saracens' was the name given to all Arabs and Muslims in the Middle Ages, though originally they were Bedouins who lived on the Turkish-Syrian border. According to some reports, the Saracens were much more civilised and chivalrous than the Christians. The Crusades - which lasted from 1095 to 1291 - ended in defeat for the Christians, who were trying to free the area which is now Palestine from the Muslims.

The passage by Lady Mary Wortley Montagu is taken from her *Letters*. In 1717, she accompanied her husband to Turkey, where he was ambassador. Her letters from Turkey include this account of her discovery of the practice of inoculation, already common practice among the Turks.

- Compare the two passages, both of which are about the treatment of ailments or diseases. You might try writing up observations in science lessons, in letters or as personal accounts like these,

Description of Cells
Robert Hooke

Hooke (1635-1703) was curator of experiments for the Royal Society (the elite group of scientists of the day), and is noted for his work in astronomy. Here, he records his observations through the recently invented microscope.

- Scientists writing up experiments often tell the story of their discoveries and observations. See if you can do the same by choosing something to look at with a microscope and recording your observations in this way.
- You might like to try an imitation or parody of Hooke's style in recording your work (eg '... methought I could perceive it to appear', 'to return to our observation' and 'I could exceedingly plainly perceive it to be ...')

Photojournalism

The other photographs in this book are of families and friends. These two, however, are of public events and are the kind that might appear in newspapers.

- Choose one of the photographs. Write a caption for it of between ten and twenty words.
- Then write a news story to accompany the photograph. Finally, give your story a headline.

Letter from a Diplomat to his Wife
Harold Nicolson

Nicolson was a British diplomat. This is a letter to his wife, Vita Sackville-West.

- Imagine yourself responding to Harold Nicolson's letter. What could you say?
- Put yourself in the shoes of someone writing home from a war front. Aim for a mix of stories, anecdotes, reflections and descriptions. Are there any letters written during a war in your family's possession? Talk to older people and collect their recollections of wartime incidents as the raw material for your own writing.

Extract from a Journal Kept whilst in Hospital
Angela Fisher

Angela Fisher is a writer living in York.
 These notes are more like the kind you would keep if you are not sitting at a desk, but writing them in bed - or on a journey, at a sports event, on holiday. That is to say, they have the feel of being put down

quickly - on the run, as it were, before the moment passes, or because there is so much to get down that you could not possibly take the long, deliberate path of composition.

- There is a difference between the beginning of the extract and the end. What is it?

The Indian Rebellion
Adelaide Case

The siege of Lucknow lasted from 1 July to 17 November 1857, during the Indian Rebellion.

- Try writing a diary under siege conditions: one in which you know that time, food, and medical resources are running out. The siege could be a military one, as in this extract, or some other survival test, such as that of plane crash victims in the Amazon, or shipwreck casualties.

One Less Octopus at Paxos
Russell Hoban

Russell Hoban is an American who started his career as an illustrator. He is the author of *Turtle Diary* and a number of children's books including *The Mouse and his Child*. Paxos is a Greek island.

- An event: the spearing and beating of an octopus. But after that, the storyteller takes you back in time to follow this woman from the moment she looks in at the travel agents' windows to 'her naked feet' and the fact a 'bystander' explained she had squirted detergent into the octopus' hiding-place. Why does Russell Hoban end with her (and us!) 'looking down at her naked feet'?
- This story is told backwards. We see the background building up to a single event. See if you could tell or write a story in this way. Start with an event (anything, from an event that you have witnessed to a large-scale public event that is currently in the news) and working from a point in the past (like looking in the travel agents' windows) trace the background to that event.

South African Journal
Barbara Webb

This is an extract from a journal written by an English visitor to South Africa. The writer kept a daily diary in note form and wrote up the journal on her return, as a way of recording and understanding her experiences. This extract recounts in a concentrated form three personal stories told to the writer by black maids or their employers.

- Working in groups of three, imagine you are using this journal extract as the basis for a 45 minute TV or radio documentary. Plan how you would do this. What will you use and what will you leave out? Will you use a narrator? Will you tell the stories directly or less directly? What locations will you use? Aim to produce a draft outlining your approach

and the main sections into which your script will divide. Then record or perform your script.
- Or you could use this text as a model for some writing of your own, in which you tell a story and then reflect upon it.

Short Stories

Most short stories are quite long compared with the writing you do in school: two thousand words is a pretty short short story; many are likely to be more than three thousand words in length. And yet often in school you will have written stories that are less than five hundred words long.

The stories in this section range from about 750 words upwards: you might like to arrange them in terms of length and see what approaches each of the writers takes. You might also like to test the suggestion that most stories are much longer than you think by calculating the length of short stories in any collection (though you'll find much shorter stories elsewhere in this collection).

Short stories tend to be fictional, in varying degrees. You might also like to list the stories in order of 'fictionality': which is the most likely to have actually happened, and which is the least likely? How do you know?

As well as the suggestions for activities for each text, here are some general ideas on short short stories:

- *Writing a short story*: you can start this in various ways, from a title, from a phrase that has struck you, from an event, or from an idea or theme you wish to explore. You can compose the story in different ways: quickly, in a first draft that is polished up later; painstakingly, over a long period of time; in one sitting, and so on. There are no rigid rules for the composition of short stories, though it is worth bearing Edgar Allen Poe's advice in mind: aim for a single effect.
- *Reading short stories*: one of the most successful ways to approach short stories (and one that is not very easy to embody in this book) is to reveal the tale bit by bit, asking for predictions as to what is going to happen as you go along. Another is to prepare cloze versions of stories, where individual words are deliberately left out and the reader has to guess what might have gone there. You can have fun devising these passages for friends to try out. In addition to these ideas, creating alternative endings to stories, interviewing characters from the stories, illustrating them, making up new titles and dramatising them are some of the approaches it is possible to take. You will be able to think of many others.

1997: The Illegal Immigrant
Isobel Jacobs

This is the work of a school student in Hong Kong, written against the background of the return of Hong Kong to China by the British in 1997. It comes from a piece in which she looks at the problem from the perspective of four characters.

- Take another situation - perhaps one that is current as you read this book - and take at least two characters who might be involved in this situation. Write an account of what is happening from the perspective of each character. The account can be a brief story, as in '1997: The Illegal Immigrant'. It will help if the characters you choose are different.
- Stories based around characters rather than around settings or plots *are* relatively rare. Make a list of the characters that stand out for you from several books you have read or films you have seen: is it what they *are* or what they *do* that is their most memorable feature?
- Make notes on a character you would like to create. He or she could be based on someone you know, or be more purely fictional. Try to make him or her different from any of the characters you already know from books or films. If you have time, create a story around this character.

Nicole and the Giant Cake
Celia Milford

This story was written by a nine-year-old girl in a Bradford school.

- There are various activities to try with this story. The simplest is to read it aloud for pleasure to an audience - a few friends, your class, or perhaps a class of junior school children.
- But it is also an interesting story for you to analyze. Find out, from a close reading of the story:
    - whether it is told in chronological order
    - whether the narrator (the voice that is telling the story) is that of a nine-year-old girl
    - what kinds of repetition it contains.
- Then stand back and decide whether you think these features work. If so, how? If not, why not?
- The story also provides a model of how to include letters in a story. You might like to try writing such a story yourself, either for people your own age, or for younger children.
- If you were going to make this story into an illustrated book for children, where would you make the page divisions?
- Find or write a story which *you* can illustrate.

The Follower
Cynthia Asquith

- We all have a favourite ghost or horror story, either one we have heard or read or a story about a ghost encountered in our own lives. Working in pairs, tell your partner a ghost story which has particularly affected you. Then try writing it in as short a form as you can, for instance, 150 words is difficult but very effective! Does your partner

think the story loses or gains by being shortened?
- Imagine that you have been commissioned to adapt 'The Follower' as a film. (Its setting, in and around the time and location of Sherlock Holmes' Baker Street, make it particularly appropriate.) How would you tell the story on film? Would you include a narrator of some kind? Where would you begin and end the story to create the greatest suspense and horror? Working in pairs, draft the order of the principal incidents on large sheets of paper.

Thank You M'am
Langston Hughes

Hughes is an American short-story writer and poet. This story was collected in *Sudden Fiction*.

- When you have read the story, discuss the following statements in a pair or small group:
  - the story is called 'Thank You M'am' because the woman gives the boy ten dollars
  - the woman and boy trust each other by the end of the story
  - this is an improbable tale: it's unlikely to happen
  - the boy probably won't steal again
  - the story could have been longer
  - it is a good story.
- Imagine the scene when Roger meets his friends and tells them about this episode. Would he pretend it hadn't happened or would he tell the truth? Try a dramatisation of the scene.

The Story of an Hour
Kate Chopin

This story comes from Kate Chopin's collection *Portraits*. Chopin was born in St Louis in 1850 and was a novelist and short-story writer. Her two novels are *At Fault* and *The Awakening*.

- Try this role-play after you have read the story twice: the doctors who come at the end speak to the three remaining characters about Louise's death (they might talk over tea in a room in the house). You will need four or five characters: a doctor; a doctor's assistant (optional); Brently; Richards; Josephine.
- You may wish to script this conversation, or to perform it after a rehearsed improvisation. Each of the characters will have his or her story to tell, and there may well be some rather disturbing revelations during the conversation (e.g. if Brently becomes aware of his wife's yearning for freedom).
- Write Louise's last diary entry, in which she reveals her frustrations and hopes about her marriage to Brently.
- Imagine that instead of dying Louise lives. Write, and then perform or record, the dialogue between Louise and Brently that takes place later that day, when the shock of his arrival has passed.

The Blue Bouquet
Octavio Paz

Paz is a Mexican poet, essayist, and short-story writer who recently won the Nobel Prize for Literature. This story is from *Eagle or Sun?*

- You are staying in a far-off country. You awake in the middle of the night and feel the need to walk out in the village or town in which you are staying. What happens? Write a story that begins in a similar way to 'The Blue Bouquet' but develops in a very different way.

An Unpleasant Reminder
Anne Kavan

This story appears in Hermione Lee's collection *The Secret Self 2*.

- What *is* 'in store' for the narrator of the story? Continue the story to solve the mystery. Aim if you can to maintain the style of the story so far. You might pick up clues from the story to help you to decide what is going to happen, what the pills are, and who the 'unknown woman' is.
- This story reads like a bad dream. Try writing down a dream you have had. It could be a nightmare or a good dream, or one of the many that seems neither good nor bad. Because dreams don't always come as straightforward stories, you might like to experiment with the way your narrative develops: is it to be fragmented and in short sections? Will it end abruptly or smoothly? Is it realistic or surreal (above and beyond what is real)?

A Story to Finish
George Orwell

Orwell (whose real name was Eric Blair) wrote essays, stories and novels during the 1930s and 1940s. His most famous novels are *Animal Farm* and *Nineteen Eighty-four*.

- Finish the story!

What a Beauty!
Theo van den Boogaard

Theo van den Boogaard is a Dutch artist. 'What a Beauty!' appeared as a postcard.

- Write a story in which three or four characters each fancy someone different in the group; and in which there is no clear-cut mutual relationship. How will the problem be resolved?

LIST OF TEXTS BY THEME

Accidents
Raymond Carver 'The Projectile'
Samuel Pepys 'The Fire of London'

Adventures
Anon 'Winnie and Walter'
Langston Hughes 'Thank You, M'am'
Octavio Paz 'The Blue Bouquet'
Celia Milford 'Nicole and the Giant Cake'

Animals
Ernest Hemingway 'Cat in the Rain'
Suniti Namjoshi 'Of Cats and Bells'
Annie Dillard 'Learning to Stalk Muskrats'

Buses (incidents on buses)
Raymond Queneau 'Notation', 'Litotes',
'Interjections', 'Official Letter',
John Cage 'The Full Bus'
Tobias Wolff 'I was on a bus to Washington, DC'

Childhood memories
Elizabeth Bentley 'Testament of a Little Doffer'
Victoria Wood 'Service Wash'
John Best 'John'
Gcina Mhlope 'The Toilet'
Iris Bradford 'I used to think babies'
Frances Cornford 'A Recollection'
Ramon Figueroa 'Solo Tackle'

Country and countryside
Annie Dillard 'Learning to Stalk Muskrats'

Creation
Bini people 'Why the Sky is Far Away'
Mayan people *from the* Popul Vuh'
Delaware Indians 'The Great Manito'

Crime and punishment
Diana Rigg 'Saturday Shopping'

Crowds and crowd behaviour
Samuel Pepys 'A Prize Fight'

Death and dying
John Best 'John'
Frances Cornford 'A Recollection'
Brett Lovell 'A Better Place'
Kate Chopin 'The Story of an Hour'
Anna Kavan 'An Unpleasant Reminder'

Faith and religion
John Best 'John'

Family
Jorge Luis Borges 'The Captive'
John Best 'John'
Maxine Hong Kingston 'On Fathers'

Fear
Octavio Paz 'The Blue Bouquet'
Anna Kavan 'An Unpleasant Reminder'
Brett Lovell 'A Better Place'

Freedom
Alexander Solzhenitsyn 'Freedom to Breathe'
Langston Hughes 'Thank You, M'am'
Kate Chopin 'The Story of an Hour'

Friendship and camaraderie
Raymond Carver 'The Projectile'

Gangs
Raymond Carver 'The Projectile'
Linda Haas 'Everyone thought he was cool and tough'

Incidents/Observations
Russell Hoban 'One Less Octopus at Paxos'
Tobias Wolff 'I was on a bus to Washington, D.C.'
Robert Hooke 'Description of Cells'
Jorge Luis Borges 'The Captive'
John Cage 'The Full Bus'
Ramon Figueroa 'Solo Tackle'

Journeys
Suniti Namjoshi 'The Giantess'

List of Texts by Theme

Journeys (continued)
Bertolt Brecht 'Travelling in a Comfortable Car'
Tobias Wolff 'I was on a bus to Washington, D.C.'

Justice
Langston Hughes 'Thank You, M'am'

Life stories
Jorge Luis Borges 'The Captive'
Victoria Wood 'Service Wash'
Dolores Dante 'I have to be a waitress'
John Best 'John'
Angela Fisher 'Extract from a Journal Kept Whilst in Hospital'
Barbara Webb 'South African Journal'

Love and relationships
Penny Maplestone 'A Cautionary Tale'
Ernest Hemingway 'Cat in the Rain'
Kate Chopin 'The Story of an Hour'

Medicine
Lady Mary Wortley Montagu 'Ingrafting the Small-pox'
Ousama 'Comparative Methods of Medicine'

Money
Fred Manley 'The Woodcutter's Son'

Persecution
Brett Lovell 'A Better Place'
Harold Nicolson 'Letter from a Diplomat to his Wife'

Politics
Pitika Ntuli 'A Story of our Times'
Isobel Jacobs '1997: The Illegal Immigrant'

Poverty and want
Bertolt Brecht 'Travelling in a Comfortable Car'
Fred Manley 'The Woodcutter's Son'

Teenagers
Linda Haas 'Everyone thought he was cool and tough'
Raymond Carver 'The Projectile'

Towns
Octavio Paz 'The Blue Bouquet'
Alexander Solzhenitsyn 'Freedom to Breathe'

Travel
Ernest Hemingway 'Cat in the Rain'
Russell Hoban 'One Less Octopus at Paxos'
Bertolt Brecht 'Travelling in a Comfortable Car'

War
Harold Nicolson 'Letter from a Diplomat to his Wife'
Adelaide Case 'The Indian Rebellion'
George Orwell 'A Story to Finish'

Weather
Anna Kavan 'An Unpleasant Reminder'
Octavio Paz 'The Blue Bouquet'
Alexander Solzhenitsyn 'Freedom to Breathe'
Ernest Hemingway 'Cat in the Rain'

Women
Maxine Hong Kingston 'On Discovery'
Suniti Namjoshi 'The Giantess'
Dolores Dante 'I have to be a waitress'
Victoria Wood 'Service Wash'

Work
Dolores Dante 'I have to be a waitress'
Elizabeth Bentley 'Testament of a Little Doffer'
Celia Milford 'Nicole and the Giant Cake'

INDEX OF AUTHORS AND ILLUSTRATORS

Anon 9
Asquith, Cynthia 84

Bentley, Elizabeth 42
Best, John 47
Bini people 24
Boogaard, Theo van den 100
Borges, Jorge Luis 17
Bradford, Iris 48
Brecht, Bertolt 29, 64

Cage, John 15
Carver, Raymond 41
Case, Adelaide 72
Chopin, Kate 90
Clarke, Bob 56
Combi, Linda 26, 36
Cornford, Frances 55

Dante, Dolores 44
Delaware Indians 22
Dillard, Annie 58
Du Li 27

Figueroa, Ramon 63
Fisher, Angela 71
La Fontaine 27

Haas, Linda 40
Hemingway, Ernest 18
Hoban, Russell 73
Hooke, Robert 68
Hughes, Langston 87

Jacobs, Isobel 78

Kavan, Anna 94

Kingston, Maxine Hong 15, 16

Logue, Christopher 62
Lovell, Brett 8

Manley, Fred 30
Maplestone, Penny 8
Mayan people 24
Mhlope, Gcina 49
Milford, Celia 79
Montagu, Lady Mary Wortley 67

Namjoshi, Suniti 28
Nicolson, Harold 71
Ntuli, Pitika 25

Orwell, George 96
Ousama 67

Paz, Octavio 92
Pepys, Samuel 65

Queneau, Raymond 13, 14

Rigg, Diana 8

Skingley, Pete 66
Solzhenitsyn, Alexander 10
Strickland, Amy 39
Swartland, Gabriel 38

Webb, Barbara 74
Wolff, Tobias 63
Wood, Victoria 59
Wu Guangxiao 27

ACKNOWLEDGEMENTS

The editors and publishers wish to thank the following who have kindly given permission for the use of copyright material:-

Art Unlimited, Amsterdam, for the drawing 'What a Beauty!' by Theo van den Boogaard.

Michael Asquith for the story 'The Follower' by Cynthia Asquith.

Basil Blackwell Publishers Ltd. for the extract 'I used to think babies ...' by Iris Bradford from *Hooligans or Rebels*, ed. Stephen Humphries.

Marion Boyars Publishers Ltd. for the story 'The Full Bus' from *Silence* by John Cage.

The Calder Educational Trust for an extract from *Exercises in Style* by Raymond Queneau, translated by Barbara Wright. Copyright © Editions Gallimard 1947. Translation copyright © Barbara Wright 1958, 1979.

Jonathan Clowes Ltd. on behalf of Doris Lessing for an extract from *Shikasta*. Copyright © Doris Lessing 1979.

E.P. Dutton Inc., an imprint of New American Library, a division of Penguin Books USA Inc. for 'The Captive' from *The Aleph and Other Stories* by Jorge Luis Borges, translated by Norman Thomas di Giovanni. Translation copyright © 1968, 1969, 1970 by Emece Editores, S.A. and Norman Thomas di Giovanni.

The Federation of Worker Writers & Community Publishers, Brighton, on behalf of Ken Jones for 'Ken Jones was a shop steward' and John Best for 'John' from *Writing*, 1978.

HarperCollins Publishers Ltd. for the story 'The Toilet' by Gcina Mhlope from *Sometimes When It Rains*, ed. Ann Oosthuisen; for 'Letter from a Diplomat to his Wife' by Harold Nicolson, from *Diaries & Letters 1939-45*, ed. Nigel Nicholson, and for an extract 'The Projectile' by Raymond Carver from *In A Marine Light*.

A.M. Heath & Co. Ltd. on behalf of the Estate of the late Sonia Brownell Orwell for 'A Story to Finish' by George Orwell, published by Martin Secker & Warburg Ltd.

Hodder & Stoughton Ltd. and Random House Inc. for an extract 'Everyone thought he was cool and tough ...' by Linda Haas from *American Dreams*, ed. Studs Terkel.

Isobel Jacobs for an extract from her story *1997 The Illegal Immigrant*.

Ewan MacNaughton Associates on behalf of Alan Sutton Publishing Ltd. and The Sunday Telegraph Ltd. for three extracts from *Mini-Sagas 2*, 'Saturday Shopping' by Diana Rigg, 'A Cautionary Tale' by Penny Maplestone, and 'A Better Place' by Brett Lovell.

Mayer, Brown & Platt on behalf of the Hemingway Foreign Rights Trust, with Charles Scribner's Sons, an imprint of Macmillan Publishing Company, New York, for 'Cat in the Rain' from *In Our Time* by Ernest Hemingway. Copyright 1925 by Charles Scribner's Sons, renewed 1953 by Ernest Hemingway. All rights outside USA with Hemingway Foreign Rights Trust.

Suniti Namjoshi for 'The Giantess' and 'Of Cats and Bells'.

Pitika Ntuli for 'A Story of our Times' from *Voices from Twentieth Century Africa*, published by Faber and Faber Ltd.

Octopus Publishing Group Ltd. for 'Service Wash' from *Up to You, Porky* by Victoria Wood, published by Methuen, London; for 'Travelling in a Comfortable Car' from *Poems 1913-1956* by Bertolt Brecht, translated by Michael Hamburger, published by Methuen, London, and 'Anecdotes of Mr. Keuner' from *Tales from the Calendar* by Bertolt Brecht, translated by Yvonne Kapp, published by Methuen, London.

Peter Owen Ltd. for an extract from *An Unpleasant Reminder* by Anna Kavan, and with New Directions Publishing Corporation, New York, for 'The Blue Bouquet' by Octavio Paz from *Eagle or Sun?* Copyright © 1976 by Octavio Paz and Eliot Weinberger.

Pan-Macmillan Books for two extracts 'On Discovery' and 'On Fathers' by Maxine Hong Kingston from *China Men* published by Picador.

Private Eye Magazine for 'True Stories' by Christopher Logue, in Vol. 731, 8th December, 1989.

Random Century Group for the poem 'A Recollection' by Frances Cornford from *Collected Poems 1954*, published by Hutchinson Publishers; for the extract 'Learning to Stalk Muskrats' from *Pilgrim at Tinker Creek* by Annie Dillard published by Jonathan Cape Ltd; for an extract from *Slaughterhouse Five* by Kurt Vonnegut, and for an extract from *Stories and Prose Poems* by Alexander Solzhenitsyn, published by The Bodley Head.

Transworld Publishers Ltd. for the jacket blurb of *Love Medicine* by Louise Erdrich.

University of Oklahoma Press for an extract from *Popul Vuh: The Sacred Book of the Ancient Quiché Maya* from the translation of Adrian Recinos. Copyright © by the Publishers.

The Women's Press Ltd. for 'The Story of an Hour' from *Portraits* by Kate Chopin.

Every effort has been made to trace all the copyright holders but if any have been inadvertently overlooked the publishers will be pleased to make the necessary arrangements at the first opportunity.

The editors would like the thank Barbara Webb, Fred Manley, Celia Milford, Isobel Jacobs, Amy Strickland and Gabriel Swartland for permission to include their work, and Paul Wagstaff, Mary Bean, Marcie Wolfe and Robert Protherough for suggestions and advice during the making of the book.

Photograph Acknowledgements

The editors and publishers wish to acknowledge, with thanks, the following photographic sources:

Camera Press Limited p 70 (top)
Sally and Richard Greenhill p 46
Popperfoto p66, 70 (bottom)